George Henry Jessop, And others

Shamus O'Brien

A Romantic Comic Opera in Two Acts, Op. 61

George Henry Jessop, And others

Shamus O'Brien

A Romantic Comic Opera in Two Acts, Op. 61

ISBN/EAN: 9783337022037

Printed in Europe, USA, Canada, Australia, Japan

Cover: Foto ©Thomas Meinert / pixelio.de

More available books at **www.hansebooks.com**

Shamus O'Brien.

A Romantic Comic Opera

in Two Acts,
Founded on the Poem
by

JOSEPH SHERIDAN LE FANU,

Written by

GEO. H. JESSOP,

Composed by

CHARLES VILLIERS STANFORD

Pianoforte Arrangement
by
MYLES B. FOSTER.

Op. 61.

Price 5/=

BOOSEY & Co.

295 Regent Street, LONDON, W.
and
9 East Seventeenth Street, NEW YORK.

Copyright 1896 by Boosey & Co

Printed by W. Eaton Long &

Contents.

Act I.

Act II.

Characters.

Opera Comique
London
March 2. 1896.

Shamus O'Brien ("on his keeping" i. e. outlawed.)   *Baritone.*   DENIS O'SULLIVAN.

Father O'Flynn (The Parish Priest of Ballybawis.)   *Bass.*   CHARLES MAGRATH.

Captain Trevor (of the British Army.)   *Tenor.*   WILLIAM STEPHENS.

Mike Murphy (a Peasant Farmer.)   *Tenor.*   JOSEPH O'MARA.

Sergeant Cox (of Captain Trevor's Company.)   FRANK FISHER.

Nora O'Brien (Wife of Shamus.)   *Mezzo Soprano.*   LOUISA KIRKBY LUNN.

Kitty O'Toole (Sister to Nora.)   *Soprano.*   MAGGIE DAVIES.

Little Paudeen (The heir of the O'Briens.)

Soldiers, Peasants, Villagers. &c.

Period. Immediately after the suppression of the rebellion of 1798.

Note.

The Composer has only used two traditional folk-songs in this opera, viz: the Irish air known as 'The Top of the Cork Road' or more commonly as 'Father O'Flynn,' and an old English March Tune of the time of Cromwell known as "the Glory of the West."

SHAMUS O'BRIEN.

Nº 1. Overture.

C. V. Stanford, Op. 61.

Allegro.

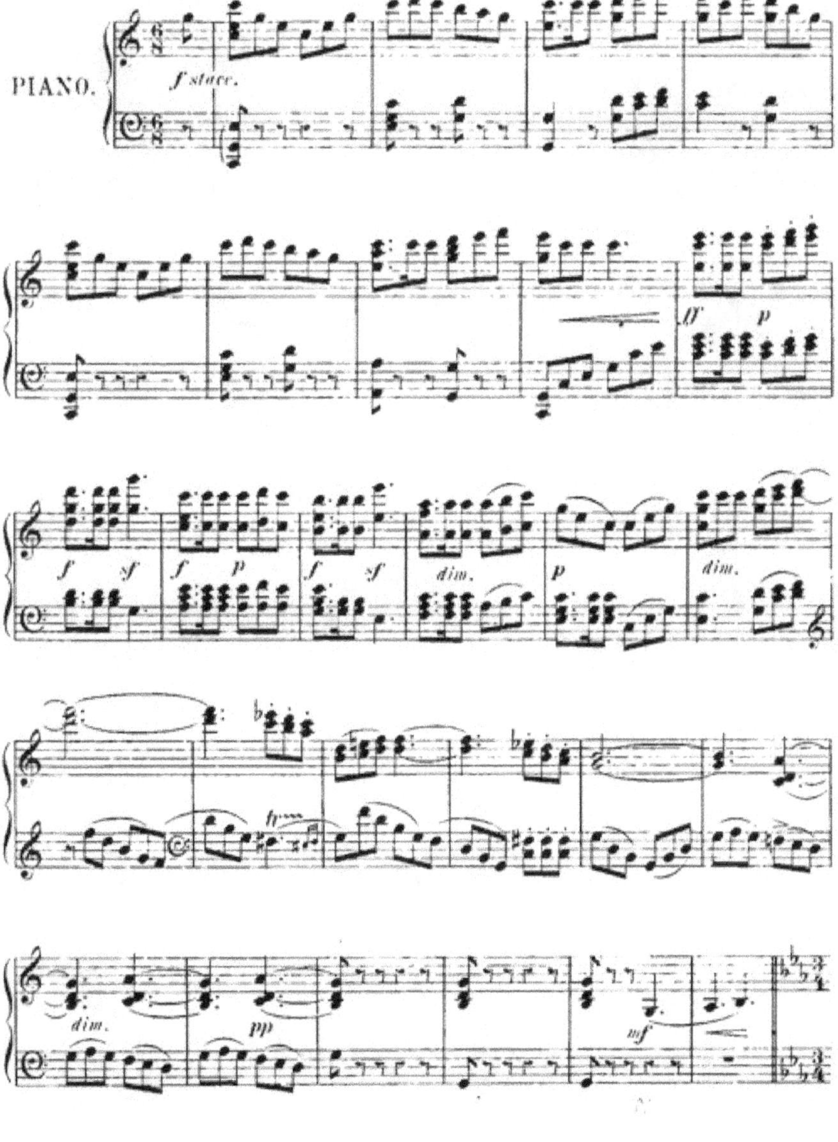

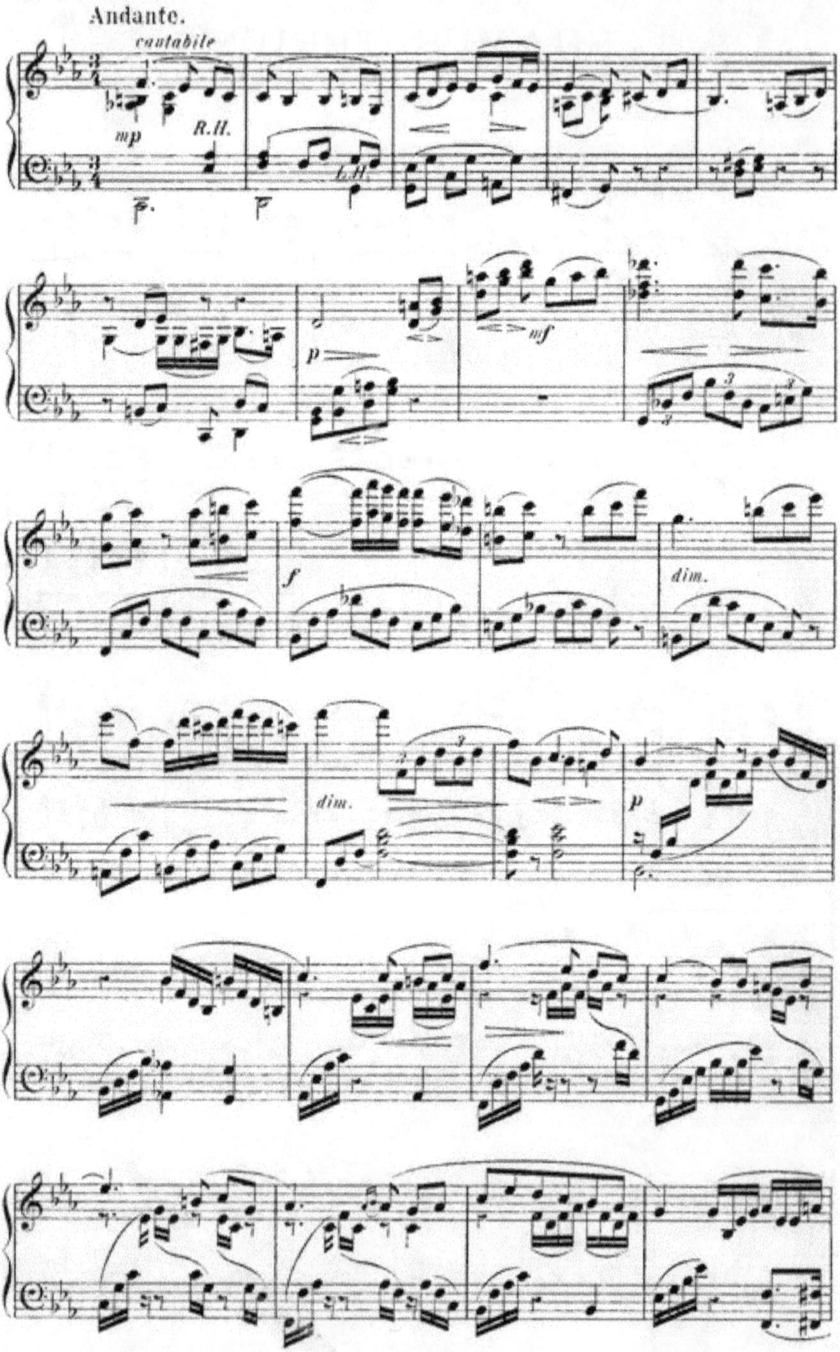
Andante.
cantabile
mp
R.H.
L.H.
p
mf
3
f
dim.
dim.
p

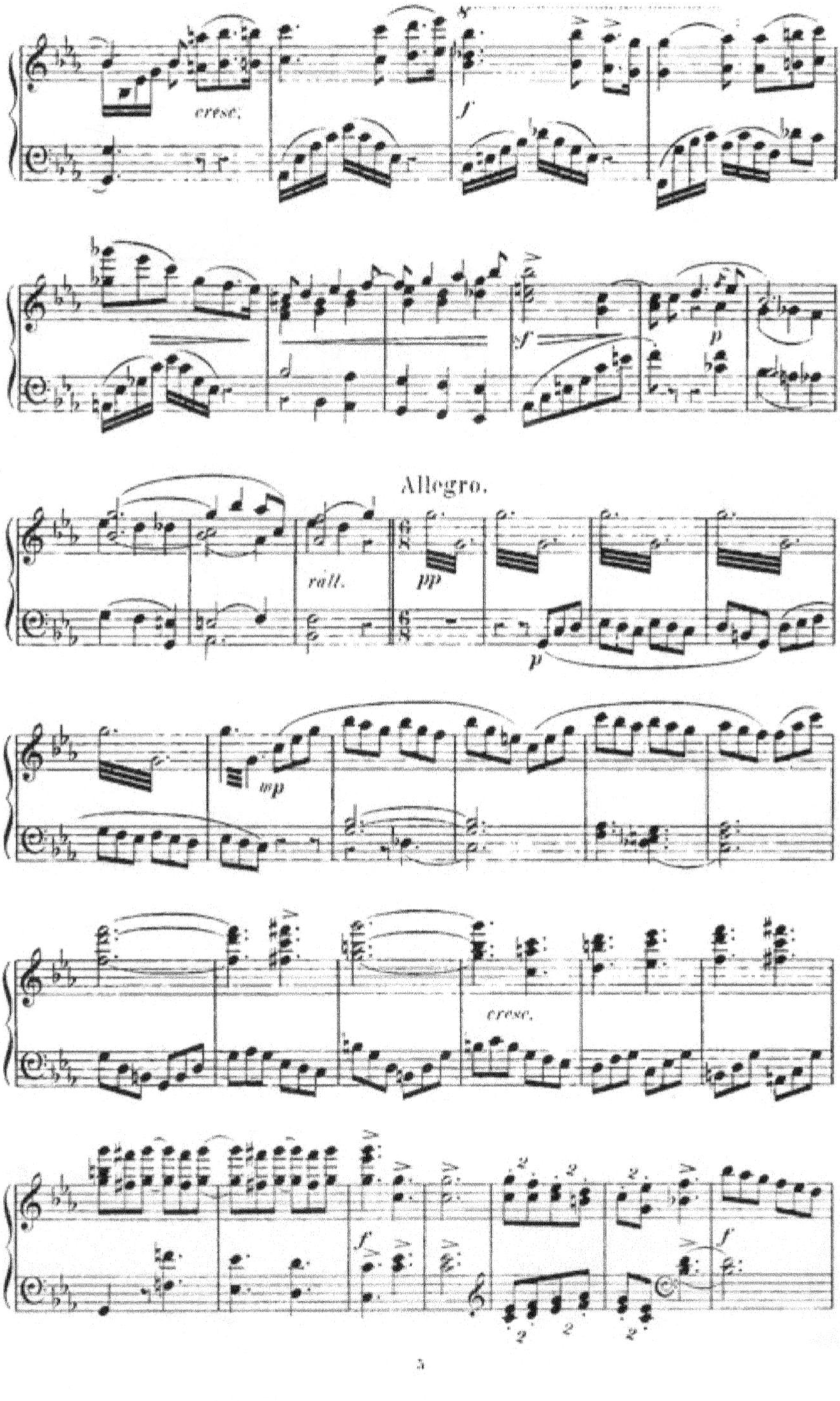
cresc.
f
Allegro.
rall.
pp
p
mp
cresc.
f
f

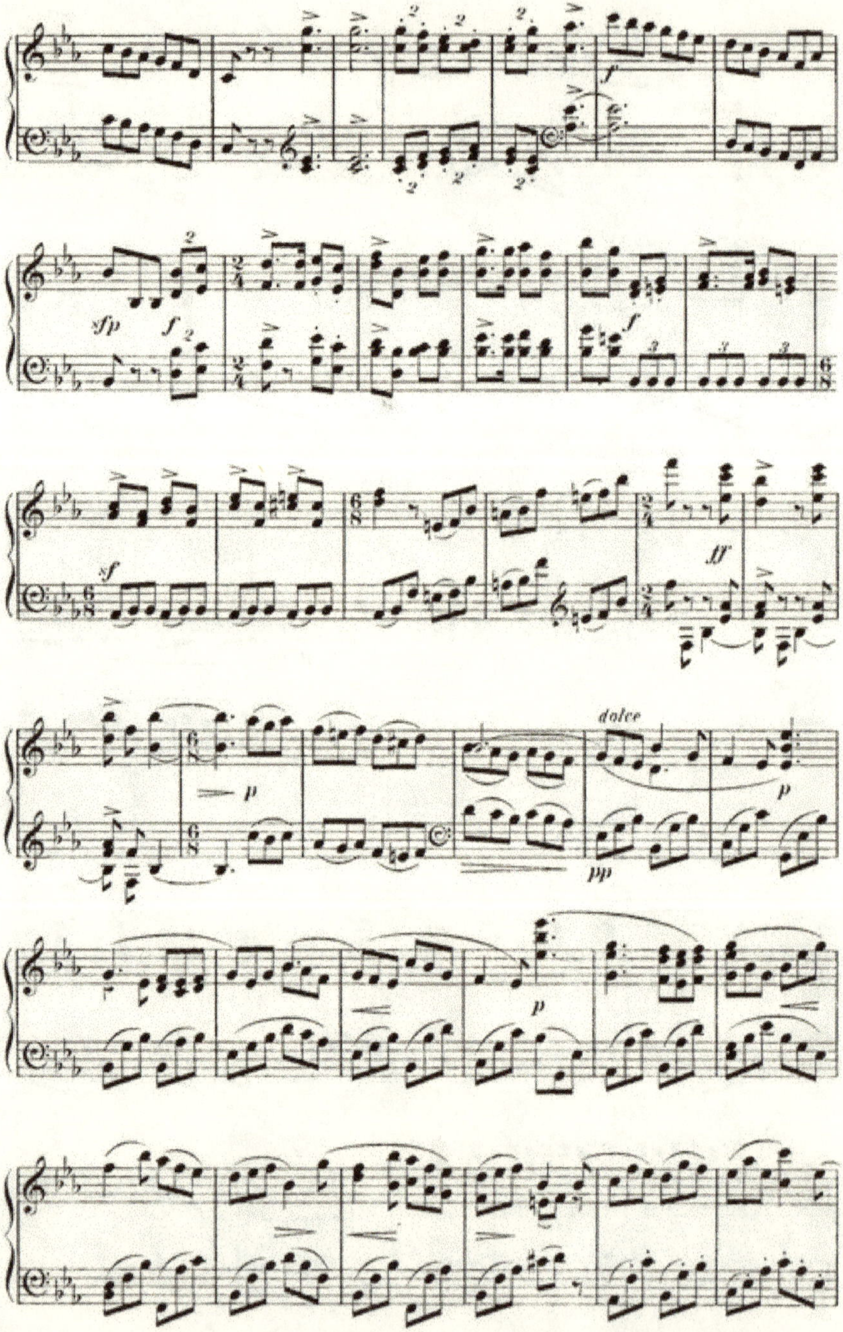
sfp
f
sf
ff
p
dolce
pp

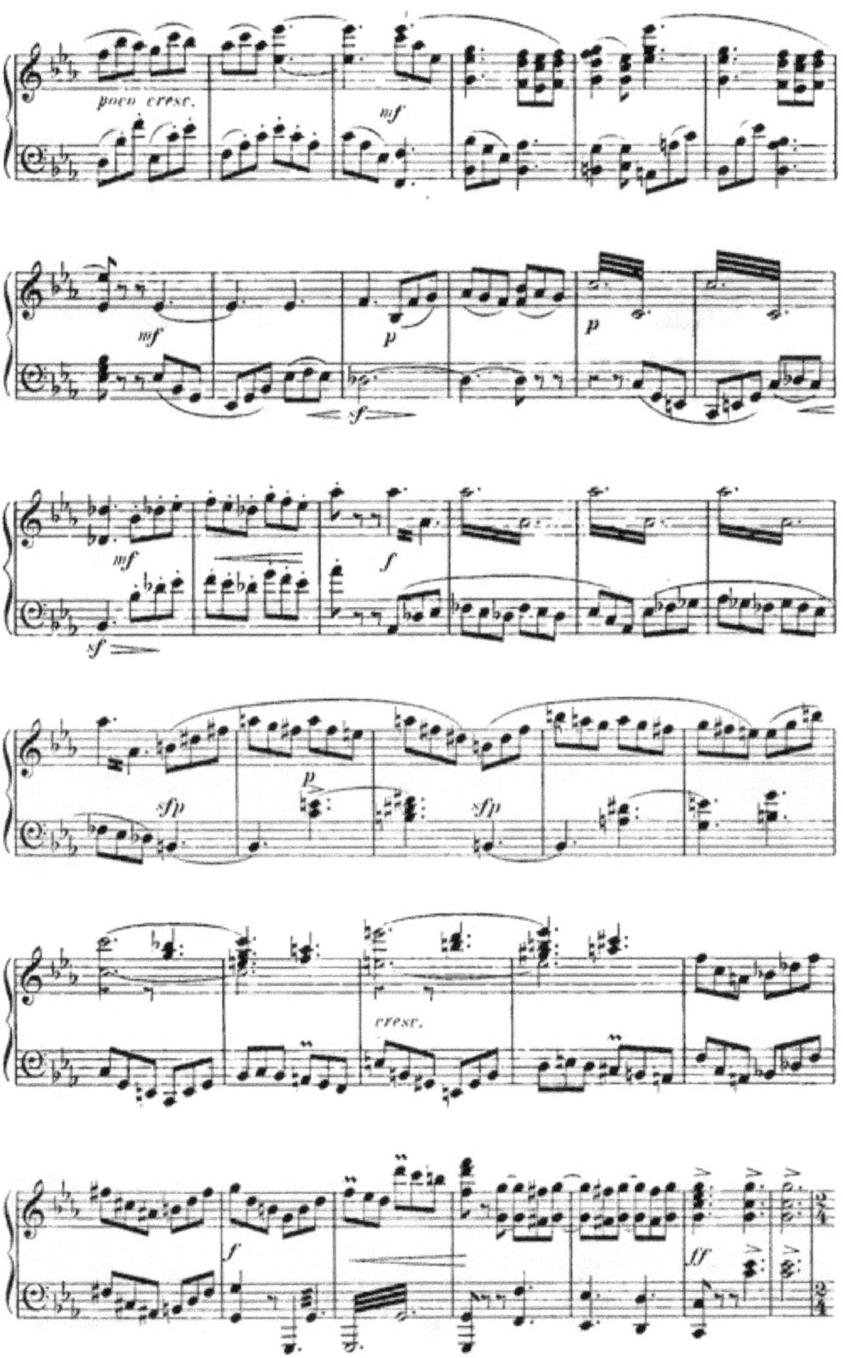
poco cresc.
mf
mf
p
p
sf
mf
sf
f
sfp
p
sfp
cresc.
f
ff

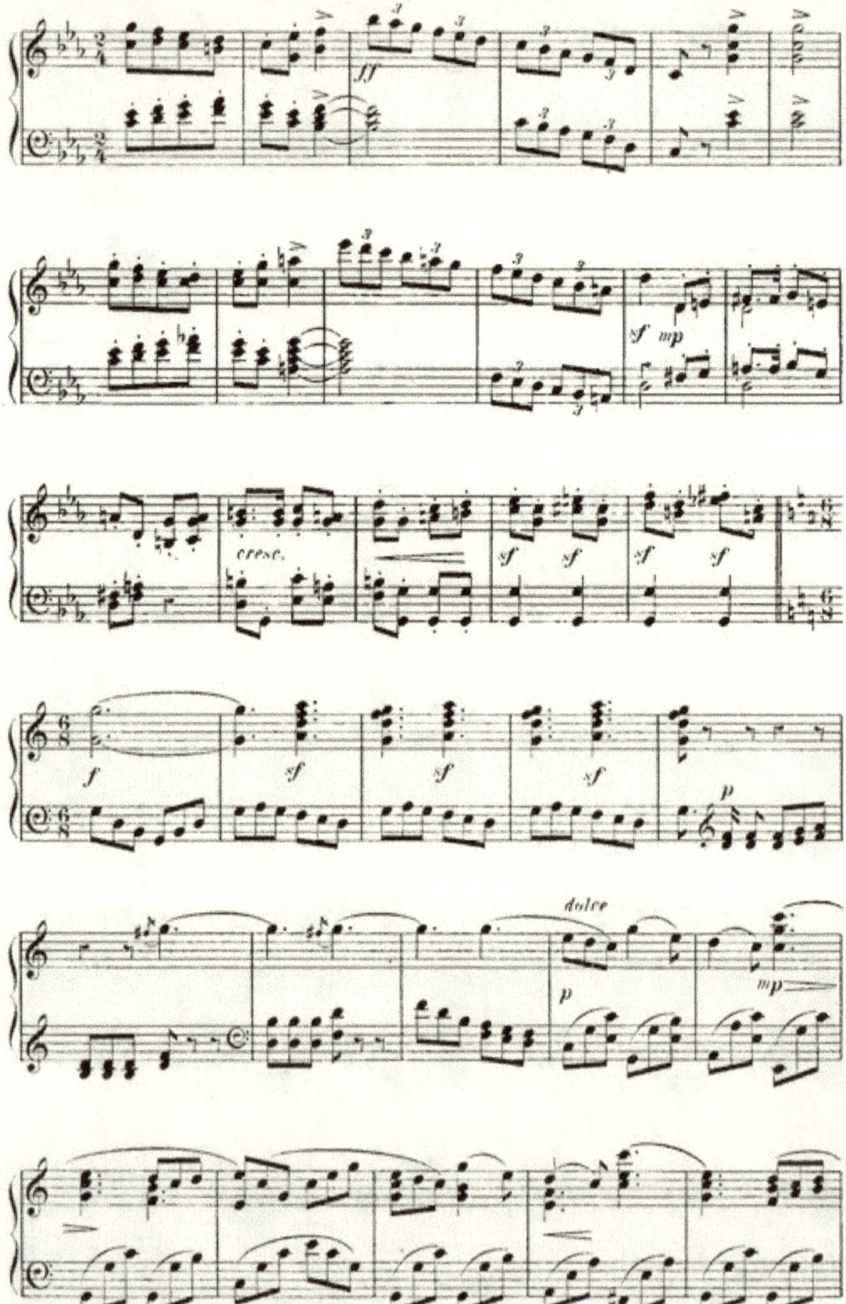
ff
sf
mp
cresc.
sf
f
p
dolce
mp

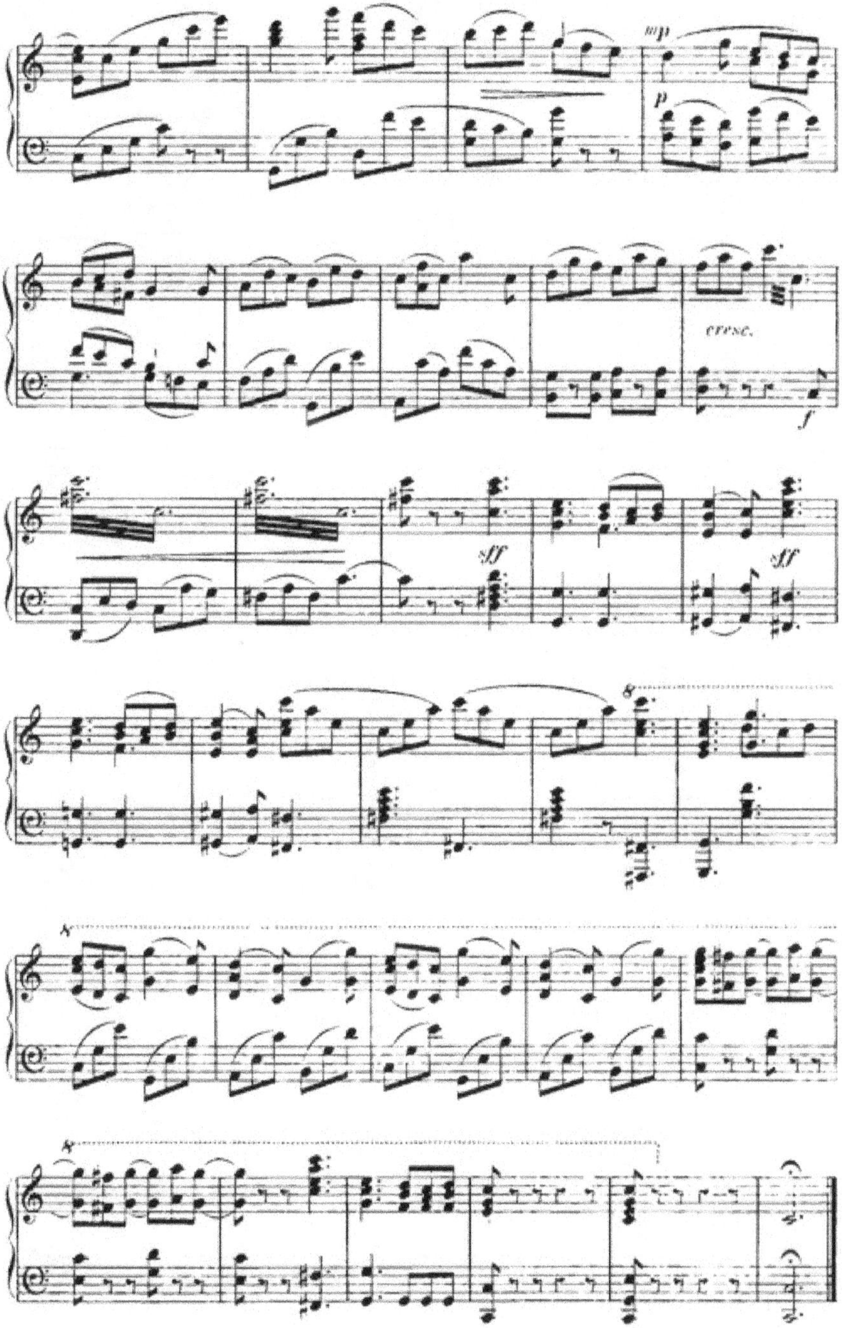
mp
p
cresc.
f
ff
ff
8

Act I.

Scene. Village of Ballyhamis, in the mountains of Cork.
Time. Immediately after the suppression of the Rebellion of 1798.

The poor village street of Ballyhamis, Shamus' cottage set 1. Door practicable. Other cabins on drop, and mountain road winding off r. c. A few set trees and other features.
(The Chorus is in two parts, which reply to each other and then come together.)

Nº 2. Chorus.
Allegro.

p stacc.   _cresc._

_mf_

(Curtain.)

Soprano.

Alto.
It's wicked news.   It's wicked news It's

Tenor.

Bass.
It's bitter news.   It's bitter news.   It's

trem _p_ _mf_

Spake up a-vick.   And tell us

cru-el news we're hear - ing.   It's bit-ter news,   It's

Spake up a-vick.   And tell us quick.

cru-el news we're hear - ing.   It's wicked news.

_p_

quick, What trouble ye are fear - ing! Spake up, spake up!
bitter news. it's wicked!
and tell us quick. What trouble ye are fear - ing!
It's wicked news, it's cru-el! Too
soon, faith ye'll know Whence is com - ing the blow. The murder, the terror, the
p
cresc.
8va ad lib.
pillage. They'll hunt him with dogs Thro' the mountains and bogs Our darlint, the pride of our
f
f
f
They'll hunt him with dogs Thro' the mountains and bogs Our dar -
Och, one! They'll hunt him with dogs Thro' the mountains and bogs Our dar -
They'll hunt him with dogs Thro' the mountains and bogs Our dar -
village! Our dar -
f
f

- lint. the pride ___ the pride of our vil-lage!

- lint. the pride ___ the pride of our vil-lage! It's

- lint. the pride ___ the pride of our vil-lage!

- lint the pride of our vil-lage! It's bit-ter news,

It's cru-el. cru-el. wick-ed. wick-ed.

wick-ed news, It's cru-el. cru-el. wick-ed. wick-ed.

It's cru-el news, cru-el. cru-el wick-ed. wick-ed.

It's cru-el news, cru-el. cru-el wick-ed. wick-ed.

Moderato.

wicked! Here's the Fath-er!

wicked! Here's the Fath - er!

wicked! Sure, he'll

wicked! Sure, he'll

Moderato.

(Enter Father O'Flynn.)

5

Trust the priest to know the news
tell us what's the mat - ter.
tell us, what's the mat - ter.
The Men uncover and bow. The Women curtsey.)
dim.
O'Flynn.
Peace be with you, peace be
dim.
with you!
Little peace, but hea - vy tidings.
p
pp
There's a blight up-on our vil-lage, and a price on Sham - us'
p
f

Tempo I.
head.
There are
It's bit-ter news,
it's wick-ed.
wick-ed!
It's bit-ter news,
it's wick-ed.
wick-ed!
It's
cru-el news.
it's
wick-ed!
It's
cru-el news.
it's
wick-ed!
wick-ed men would sell him,
though I know, good souls, you
love him and would guard him and pro-tect him,
for you know the man he
Andante.
is!
I'll

give ye to next Michaelmas to name us A gossoon so presen-table and famous, So

loved in all the neigh-bour-hood as Sha - - - mus Faith, ye

wouldn't find his match in twice as long. At

hur - ling, it's give in he bates the de-vil, He'll lep yez either high or on the

level, He's the fairest,hardest drinker at a revel,And an il-ligant performer at a song.

If Ro-mu-lus and Ra-mus Had lived a-long with Sha-mus They'd be

If Ro-mu-lus and Ra-mus Had lived a-long with Sha-mus They'd be

If Ro-mu-lus and Ra-mus Had lived a-long with Sha-mus They'd be

If Ro-mu-lus and Ra-mus Had lived a-long with Sha-mus They'd be

like two pup-py jackals with a lion: Spake up now. can you blame us. If the

like two pup-py jackals with a lion: Spake up now. can you blame us. If the

like two pup-py jackals with a lion: Spake up now. can you blame us. If the

like two pup-py jackals with a lion: Spake up now. can you blame us, If the

boys of Bal-ly-ha-mis Shout "Faugh a ballagh" Shamus The O'- Brien!

boys of Bal-ly-ha-mis Shout "Faugh a ballagh" Shamus The O'- Brien!

boys of Bal-ly-ha-mis Shout "Faugh a ballagh" Shamus The O'- Brien!

boys of Bal-ly-ha-mis Shout "Faugh a ballagh" Shamus The O'- Brien!

Ah! The colleens swear there ne'er was such a dancer, No lawyer ev-er shook him for an answer, In court one day, bowld counsellor Mc. Cann, sir. Give him up and fair-ly owned he had him bet. He wouldn't drop his eyes in front of Ne-ro, Nor tremble if the cowld was down to Zero, He's the moral and the model of a hero, He's the making and the shaping of a

poco rall.   a tempo

f   colla voce   a tempo
sfp

Pet

If Ro-mu-lus and Ra-mus Had lived a-long with Sha-mus, They'd be

like two pup-py jackals with a lion; Spake up now, can you blame us, If the

boys of Bal-ly-ha-mis Shout "Faugh a ballagh" Shamus The O'-Brien!

He never left a friend that wanted trating, He

più mosso never quit a foe that needed bating, He *più lento* never kept a boy or girl a-wait-

a tempo -ing, Wheth-er kiss-es or shil-le-laghs was the play.

cresc. He's a footfall like the red deer on the mountain, An eye like a young salmon in the

fountain. He's a way of going straight and never counting How many or how few is in his

way!
If Ro-mu-lus and Ra-mus Had lived a-long with
If Ro-mu-lus and Ra-mus Had lived a-long with
If Ro-mu-lus and Ra-mus Had lived a-long with
If Ro-mu-lus and Ra-mus Had lived a-long with
Sha-mus. They'd be like two pup-py jackals with a lion: Spake
Sha-mus. They'd be like two pup-py jackals with a lion Spake
Sha-mus. They'd be like two pup-py jackals with a lion. Spake
Sha-mus. They'd be like two pup-py jackals with a lion: Spake
up now, can you blame us, If the boys of Bal-ly-ha-mis Shout
up now, can you blame us, If the boys of Bal-ly-ha-mis Shout
up now, can you blame us. If the boys of Bal-ly-ha-mis Shout
up now, can you blame us. If the boys of Bal-ly-ha-mis Shout

"Faugh a ballagh Shamus The O-Brien.

The O'-Brien!

Faugh a ballagh Shamus The O-Brien.

The O'-Brien!

"Faugh a ballagh Shamus The O-Brien.

The O'-Brien!

"Faugh a ballagh Shamus The O-Brien.

The O'-Brien!

(cue) Kitty. "I heard all ye were saying."

Sortie.

Nº 2 (bis.)

Allegro come al 1mo.

Kitty "I think, boys, ... if they come"

Chorus.

Sop.
Let the ar - my come on With its sword and its gun To

Alt.
Let the ar - my come on With its sword and its gun To

Ten.
Let the ar - my come on With its sword and its gun To

Bass.
Let the ar - my come on With its sword and its gun To

5

har-ry and burn Bal-ly-ha-mis: A man has to
creep To catch wea-sels a-sleep.They'll as soon catch a wea-sel as
Shamus.

Kitty. "I can keep ....
...... warning"

No 3. Song.
Andante molto moderato.

Kitty "Know if ....
... Troth, will I"

"Its too much ....
... who never comes"

pp

Ped.

❋

mf Kitty.

Where is the man that is

com-ing to mar-ry me? Where is the gos-soon thats eag-er to court?

Time runs to wast-ing. the long-er I tar-ry me,

5

Age comes so surely and youth is so short. When is he coming, the

hand-some, the sun-ny-eyed, Swearing he holds me the dearest and best, ___ Just for my-

self for of course if I'd money, I'd have me grand lov - er as well as the

rest.

Boys come to coort with a kiss an' a pet to it. Never a one that I feel I could choose,

Poco più lento.

Yet I've a heart, if they on-ly could get to it. Yet I've a tongue that don't want to re-

fuse. Somewhere far off in the world, out o'sight o'me, Wait-the one as soon will

accel. poco a poco e cresc.

suit me, I know. Come, heart to heart, hand in hand, take howld

tight _____ o'me; I'll be yer bail that ye won't let me

(At the close of song Kitty bends forward in listening attitude, looking down the road, then draws back, partly out of sight behind a set tree. Voices off, and Captain Trevor and Mike Murphy enter.)

go.

(cue) Capt. Trevor. "You need not appear?"

Nº 4. Trio.

Andante leggiero.

Mike.

He's as
straight as a dart, and as slim as a rush, With a
step like a fawn, and a voice like a thrush; And his
eyes are like fire, some-times soft, some-times bright,
And the keen-fang-èd hound has-n't teeth half so

5

Kitty. *mf*

If I knew other men As handsome as he, I'd be

Capt. Trevor. *mf*

He is good looking then?

white.

axing them when?"

mf Good - looking enough for to force me to part From the

on - ly col - leen ev - er reached to my heart. But

But

But

hand-some or no, He has stri-cken a blow in the ranks of re-bellion. And

hand-some or no, He has stri-cken a blow in the ranks of re-bellion, And

hand-some or no, He has stri-cken a blow in the ranks of re-bellion. And

now he must go. Ev'-ry charm, ev'-ry grace of his fig-ure or

now he must go. Ev'ry charm ev'ry grace of his figure or face Must be noted,

now he must go. Ev'ry charm ev'ry grace of his figure or face Must be

face _____ Must be no - ted to give his pur - suers a

must be no - ted, must be no-ted to give his pur-suers a

no - - ted, must be no-ted to give his pur - suers a

Tempo I. (♩=♩ previous.)

trace.

trace. 'Tis hard, 'Tis hard that stern du-ty should

trace.

force me to part This gallant young life from the love of his

heart. **Mike.** And hard - - er to think that a trivial re-

But the money is there?

ward Should win a success I had sought_ with the sword. 'Tis

But the money is there?

Kitty

It's myself will take care 'Twill be

hard,   'tis   hard!

But the money is there?   But the money is there?___

cresc.

melted and pour'd down your throat at the fair.   It's myself will take care,

A slight, ac - tive   man   in the house with the

It's myself will take care.

doors?   When   the out - law is   taken,   the blood-money's

But the money is there?

5

Allegretto.

But hand-some or no, he has strick-en a

yours. But hand-some or no, he has strick-en a

But hand-some or no, he has strick-en a

Allegretto.

blow in the ranks of re-bellion, and now he must go! Ev'-ry charm, Ev'-ry

blow in the ranks of re-bellion, and now he must go! Ev'-ry charm, Ev'-ry

blow in the ranks of re-bellion, and now he must go! Ev'-ry charm, Ev'-ry

pp stacc.

grace both of fig - ure and face, of fig - ure and

grace both of fig - ure and face, of fig - ure and

grace both of fig - ure and face, of fig - ure and

face _____ is a sign that stern du - ty com - pels him to

face _____ is a sign that stern du - ty com - pels me to

face _____ is a sign that stern du - ty com - pels him to

trace.   'Twill be melted and pour'd down your throat at the

trace.   'Tis hard!   But   du - ty   com -

trace.   But the money is there?

fair.   'Twill be melted and pour'd down your throat at the

pels _____ me,   Yes,   du - ty   com-

But the money is there?

fair.

pels.   (angrily)
When the out-law is

But the money is there?

'Tis myself will take care____

taken the blood____ money's yours!
The blood money's there.____

So the money is there.____

...'twill be melted and pour'd down your throat at the fair.

Nº 5. Duet.

Allegretto.

Kitty.

Captain.

Well, he'd take me by the hand_ D'ye understand? And stand

close to where I stood. if he could; And he'd say, "My dar-lint Kitty, sure the

whole world knows ye're pretty, and ye're daint-y, and ye're wit-ty and ye're

good. Yes, he should.

Oh, he would? But when I-rishmen de-ceive,

5

Do you believe? Can you know what's said to you, False or true? For your

Paddy or your Barney.Tho' you're lovely as Killarney,May have taken trips to Blarney Not a

Wir-ras-thrue! Wir-ras-thrue!

few. Don't be blue! Don't be blue! For you're

Faith, he's coming on at last! Whisht! ye

grace-ful and you're winning. And when love is just beginning...

talk of love too fast, For there's many a word to pond - er, And there's

For there's many a word to pond - er, And there's

many a mile to wan - der, Ere love meets us ov - er yon - - -

many a mile to wan - der, Ere love meets us ov - er yon - - -

- der, And com - pletes the spell he cast.

- der, And com - pletes the spell he cast. (Captain touches his cap

And you're go - in' af - ter that?

and is about to go.)

Du - ty

Oh, you needn't touch your hat. I could keep you if I tried. But it
(salutes)
calls me from your side.

natural born idiot can't be taught to read his book. And a natural born Saxon can't be

taught by love or look.

Oh, demmit! pretty Kitty, if you could but read my

heart, You'd not censure, you would pity. When you see me forced to part.

poco rall.

Let me take you by the hand *As you stand! Let me taste a honey sip*

Più mosso.

I'm not ready for your tasting. So your time you're only wasting. (He attempts again and

(Captain attempts to kiss her, she repulses him.)

From your lip.

Più mosso.

poco rall. *a tempo*

You're a goose in need of basting... *Come now, stip!*

she boxes his ear.)

What a slip! *Foil'd this trip!*

a tempo

poco rall.

Never mind the reason why!

If it were not for stern duty. *I would tame you, saucy*

* Box on the ear on this note.   5

Well, I'll larn ye by and bye! For I find you'll need a les-son, Which I'll

beauty. For I find you'll need a lesson, Which I'll give you with a

give you with a blessin', with a blessin', Ere my thir-sty lips are pres-sin'

blessin', with a blessin', with a blessin', Ere my thir-sty lips are pres-sin'

on the lips, on the lips, of such as

on the lips, on the lips you hold so

high: What a slip! What a slip!

1. Come now, stip! Come now, stip! stip!
(going)

(spoken and with a stamp)

Nº 6. Song, Chorus and Ensemble.

Allegro molto e con brio.

Shamus.

I've sharpen'd the sword for the sake of ould Erin, I carried a pike when she called on her sons; I ran the risk then, and I will not be fear-in' The e-nemy's gallows no more nor his guns. The land that bred me and my colleen with-in it Has sure-ly a claim to the life that it gave; I'd

sooner be cowld on its green sod this minute, Than live an in - former, or tremble a
slave.
But life I won't yield Like a
poor panting dumb thing, Held fast in the snare or bound tight by the rope; God
put this stout heart in my bosom for something, As long as it beats, it is beating with
hope.
I'll live for my
cresc.
trem.

coun - - try. I'll live for my No - ra, I'll live for my

gos-soon, my lit-tle Pau-deen; They'll seek ere they

un poco sostenuto il

tempo

find me, they'll fight ere they score a de-feat for O'-Brien,____

And low - - - er the green!

rall.   *a tempo*

5

Call the neighbours. Call the neighbours! Put the creel u - pon the

Kitty. *f*

Men of the hillside! Ga - ther, ga -

thatch.

sfp

(Nora comes out of house carrying
Allegro non troppo.

ther! Shamus needs ye with des - patch!

mf *sf* *sf* *f presante*

8ve ad lib.

a large basket; O'Flynn follows her with a short step-ladder, which he places against the house. Nora as-

mf *sf* *mf*

cends and puts the basket on the roof.)

f *f* *cresc.* *ff* *sf* *sf*

5

42

Nora.
Come, boys, come. Throw down the scythe and spade; Come, boys,

come, Ye must learn a - no-ther trade; For ye say there's a

man That ye love more than all — 'Tis the head of your clan That is sounding the

Kitty

Nora.
Come, boys, come, throw down the scythe and spade;
call. _____
Come, boys, come, throw down the scythe and spade;

Shamus.
Come, boys, come, throw down the scythe and spade;

Father O'Flynn.
Come, boys, come, throw down the scythe and spade;

5

Come, boys, come. There's no time to be de - layed,
Come, boys, come. There's no time to be de - layed,
Come, boys, come. There's no time to be de - layed,
Come, boys, come. There's no time to be de - layed,
Bring the sticks ye've tried in smiting, Bring the girls that ye de - light in, Till they
Bring the sticks ye've tried in smiting, Bring the girls that ye de - light in, Till they
Bring the sticks ye've tried in smiting, Bring the girls that ye de - light in, Till they
Bring the sticks ye've tried in smiting, Bring the girls that ye de - light in, Till they
(Enter Chorus.)
see O'Briens fighting. Faugh a ballagh! who's a - fraid?
see O'Briens fighting. Faugh a ballagh! who's a - fraid?
see O'Briens fighting. Faugh a ballagh! who's a - fraid?
see O'Briens fighting. Faugh a ballagh! who's a - fraid?
L.H.
dim.

From the moor, from the hill, From the mea-dow and field,

From the moor, from the

hill, from the mea-dow and field, We are come, as ye will, for a sword or

We are come, as ye will, for a sword or

We are come, we are come. So the

We are come, We are come, we are come. So the

shield. We are come. So the

shield. We are come. So the

English-man wants ye? Well, if he in - sists. He'll meet good I - rish

English-man wants ye? Well, if he in - sists. He'll meet good I - rish

English-man wants ye? Well, if he in - sists. He'll meet good I - rish

English-man wants ye? Well, if he in - sists. He'll meet good I - rish

Ni. ad lib.

black-thorns. in good I - rish fists.

black-thorns. in good I - rish fists.

black-thorns. in good I - rish fists.

black-thorns. in good I - rish fists.

ff

Shamus. *f*

I know. I know.

dim.

p

5

46

Allegretto molto moderato.

Nora. *mf*

Oh, boys, listen to Shamus!

mp
I know ye are brave as brave can be — Ye'd

p *pp*

Boys, boys, who wouldn't for Sha-mus?

fight to the last for mine and me. I

know that ye'd none of you question or carp, Ye'd play on their skulls as I'd play on a harp;

rall. *a tempo* Nora. Oh,

But tho' blackthorn is tough, sure the bay-on-et's sharp!

fp *pp*

Ped. ✳

5

boys, lis-ten to Sha-mus!

I'll

Chorus Basses.

Oh, boys, lis-ten to Sha - mus!

Boys, none is wi - ser than Sha-mus!

have no fighting for me the day, Just

Boys, boys, trust it to Sha - mus!

on-ly support me in all I say. An'

I'll be your bail that I give them the talk, For I'm a red deer that they

pp

cresc.

never shall stalk:_____ An' if they want ex - er-cise, faith, they shall walk

sfp *sfp*

Kitty. *f*

Yes, boys, walk af-ter Sha - mus!

Nora. *f*

Yes, boys, walk af-ter Shamus, Yes, boys, walk af-ter Sha - mus!

O'Flynn. *f*

Yes, boys, walk af-ter Sha - mus!

Chorus.

Ten. and Bass.
mf

We'll do as he bids us.

p *p*

mf
Oh, boys, list-en to Sha-mus! For his wit is quick, and his
Chorus.
Oh, boys, list-en to Sha-mus! For his wit is quick, and his
ne-ver fear.
ne-ver fear.
p
Kitty.
There's a sea-son to fight and a
Nora.
There's a sea-son to fight and a
Shamus.
There's a sea-son to fight and a
O'Flynn.
There's a sea-son to fight and a
head is clear.
head is clear.
f
Girls, girls, listen to Sha-mus.
Girls, girls, listen to Sha-mus.

time to lie low; And we have a plan, as we'll soon let ye know. That'll

give us a laugh in the face of the foe.

Boys, boys, leave it to

Boys, boys, leave it to Sha-mus!

Boys, boys, leave it to Sha-mus!

Boys, boys, leave it to Sha-mus!

Boys, boys, leave it to Sha-mus!

Boys, boys, leave it to

Boys, boys, leave it to

Sha-mus! Boys, boys, leave it to

Sha-mus! Boys, boys, leave it to

(Two Scouts come running on R.C., shouting. — 1st Scout."Hi! hi! The soldiers! They're coming down the road!" 2nd Scout."The soldiers. The soldiers they're close upon us now!"

him!

him!

him!

him!

Tempo di marcia.

mp
Hark! Hark! Their
p
Hark!
p
Hark!
p
Their steps I'm countin', The foot - falls of sol - die-ry
p
Their steps I'm countin', The foot - falls of sol - die-ry
The foot - falls of sol - die-ry
steps I'm countin'. The foot - falls of sol - die-ry
p
Hark!
p
Hark!
p pp
Hark! Their steps I'm countin'.
p pp
Hark! Their steps I'm countin'.

(Shamus, Nora and Kitty enter the house.)

o - ver the mountain.

o - ver the mountain.

o - ver the mountain.

o - ver the mountain.

Curse on the

Curse on the

Curse on the for-eigner coming to har-ry us,

Curse on the for-eigner coming to har-ry us,

ru-in his ba-yonets car-ry us.

ru-in his ba-yonets car-ry us.

Is it a sin that our dar-lint, our Sha-mus, Drew a good

Is it a sin that our dar-lint, our Sha-mus, Drew a good

Is it a crime, a crime in the
Is it a crime, a crime in the
sword when he wanted to tame us?
sword when he wanted to tame us?

coun - try that bred us Lov - ing its hills an' its rocks an' its
coun - try that bred us Lov - ing its hills an' its rocks an' its
Lov - ing its hills an' its rocks an' its
Lov - ing its hills an' its rocks an' its

meadows? Is it a treason that all Bal - ly - ha - mis Glo - ries to own a true
meadows? Is it a treason that all Bal - ly - ha - mis Glo - ries to own a true
meadows? Is it a treason that all Bal - ly - ha - mis Glo - ries to own a true
meadows? Is it a treason that all Bal - ly - ha - mis Glo - ries to own a true

pa - triot like Sha - mus?

pa - triot like Sha - mus?

pa - triot like Sha - mus?

pa - triot like Sha - mus?

(Soldiers enter, led by Captain and Sergeant.)

Serg. "Halt! front!"

Capt. "I am in search of a rebel" &c.

5

(cue) Captain: "Demmit! This O'Brien must be somewhere, though."

Nº 7. Trio. Chorus.

Allegretto.

5

mf
If you know, you must
Ha! ha! He's the boy that knows!
Ha! ha! He's the boy that knows!
ha! Ha! ha! ha! ha! He's the boy that knows!
ha! Ha! ha! ha! ha! He's the boy that knows!
f
p
tell! You know where he'll hide?
You'll be paying me well? Ha! ha! ha!
mf
Well, I'll
ha! As if I was in - side of the gossoon him - self.
p
Ha! ha! ha!
Ha! ha! ha!
Ha! ha! ha!
Ha! ha! ha!
pp
p

give you your pelf, and en-gage you as guide.

ha!

ha!

ha!

ha!

Ha! ha!   Ha! ha!

Ha! ha!   Ha! ha!

Ha! ha!   Ha!

Ha! ha!   Ha!

We'll get ready to start.   Now, good

He'll engage meas guide!   Ha!

He'll en-gage him as guide!

He'll en-gage him as guide!

ha!   He'll en-gage him as guide!

ha!   He'll en-gage him as guide!

folks stand a - part, stand a - part, stand a - part!
ha! ha! ha!
He'll en - gage him as
He'll engage him as guide!
guide!
We'll
He'll engage him as guide! Ha! ha! Ha! ha! Him as guide!
Ha! ha! Ha! ha! Him as guide!
He'll engage him as guide! Ha! ha! Ha! ha! Him as guide!

mp ad lib.
You
look for Shaun, he left at dawn To search the bogs for a Le - prechaun.
mp colla voce
fool! You don't know e'en his name!
(smilingly)
Sure, all the world
— knows Tha - dy Farrell!
Well, I don't know him all the same.
Sure,
Sure, all the world — knows Tha - dy
Sure, all the world — knows Tha - dy
Sure, all the world — knows Tha - dy
Sure, all the world — knows Tha - dy
p
pp
f
pp
mf

E-
if ye don't, we need not quarrel! The fairies dance when they've the chance
Farrell!
Farrell!
Farrell!
Farrell!
nough of this! Point out the way! D'ye know where
A Le - prechaun, if caught at dawn
these demnid rebels lay? Point
I'm close to them where'er they go.

out the way, Point out the way if that is so.

In troth, I ought to

He's close to them!

He's close to them!

He's close to them!

He's close to them!

know!

Do ye

Ha! ha! Ha! ha! In troth he ought to know!

Ha! ha! Ha! ha! In troth he ought to know!

Ha! ha! Ha! ha! In troth he ought to know!

Ha! ha! Ha! ha! In troth he ought to know!

Andante.

know the town of Glen-gall. Where the sol - diers' barracks were?

Andante.

ought!   So I thought.   But you'll hardly find Sha - nus there!

(Captain stamps impatiently.)

Do you   know   where the bog-road   passes   By the

side of the deep   mo - rasses?   Good for   you!   For he's

Yes, I   do.

5

I want to know which
not ly-ing hid in the grasses.
way to go. And not the place he is-n't!
Ochone! och-
one! ye'd lose your pret-ty shoes In search-ing for a pisint!
Ochone! ye'd
Ochone! ye'd

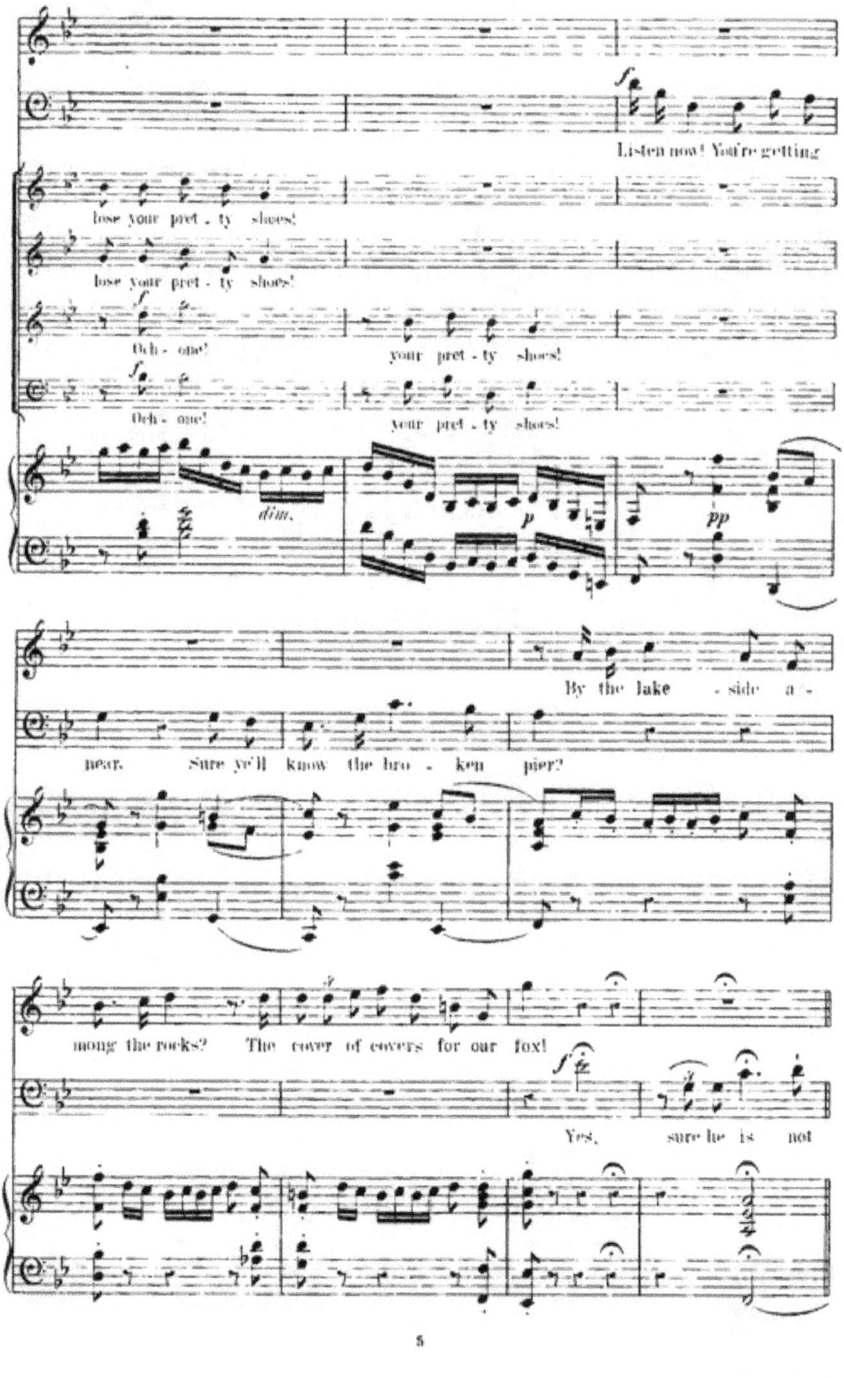

Più mosso.
Capt.
Shamus.
He is-n't there? You'd best be-ware How you in-sult me further! You'd best beware! You'd best beware!
there!
He's an-gry now, wow wow wow wow wow wow! he'll have my life!
He'll have my life — och murther! och murther! och mur-
you'd best be-
Più mosso.
Chorus
He's an-gry now, he's an-gry,
He's an-gry now,

Allegro.
ware!
Oh! he must be-have! He's be-yond all rule,
- - ther!
He's an - gry!
He's an - gry!
He's an - gry!
He's an - gry!
Allegro.
p
I pre-fer a knave — Take a-way the fool!
mf
Now your honour's quare — Spiteful as a mule. Sure, I
Shamus.
spake your fair, use me as your tool!
O'Flynn.
mp
Sure, the gos-soon's pride Shows he's not a fool, and to
mf
pp
8va ad lib.

Capt.
Oh, he must be-have, he's be-yond all rule.
Shamus.
Now your hon - our's quare,_ Spiteful as a mule,
O'Flynn.
track or guide he's a per-fect jool ______ his pride show's he not a fool, and to
sfp
pp
I pre-fer a knave Take a-way the fool.____ Take a-way the
Sure I spake you fair use me as your tool.____
track and guide he's a per - fect jool ____ he's a per - fect
To track or guide on mountain side ______
To
Chorus.
To track or guide on mountain side ______
To

fool! Take a-way the fool!
spiteful as a mule!
fool!
cresc.
to seek or hide from friends or foes.
track or guide on mountain side
to seek or hide from
to seek or hide from friends or foes
track or guide on mountain side
to seek or hide from
cresc.
from friends or foes. He's the boy, the boy that
friends or foes. or foes. He's the boy, the boy that
from friends or foes. He's the boy, the boy that
friends or foes. or foes. He's the boy, the boy that

Più lento.
Take away the fool!
take away the fool!
ad lib.
I went at
He's a perfect jool!
a
jool!
knows, He's the boy, the boy that knows, He's the boy that knows!
knows, He's the boy, the boy that knows, He's the boy that knows!
knows, He's the boy, the boy that knows, He's the boy that knows!
knows, He's the boy, the boy that knows, He's the boy that knows!
Più lento.
ff
pp
colla voce
Shamus
pp
dawn to ga-ther sloes with a Leprechaun_
He knows!
He knows!
O'Flynn.
f
He knows!
f
He knows!
f
He knows!
f
He knows!
f
He knows!
pp
f

5

But to fight or court, Potheen's what we swim in.

But to fight or court, Potheen's what we swim in.

But to fight or court, Potheen's what we swim in.

But to fight or court, Potheen's what we swim in.

Nora.

Come, boys, here's the stuff to set your hearts a-beating; Step up, take enough,

Kitty.

Bring your noggins here, See that none want filling. Liquor can't be dear

Nora.

Sure,'tis Shamus treating. Bring your noggins here, See that none want filling. Liquor can't be dear

O'Flynn.

Bring your noggins here, See that none want filling. Liquor can't be dear

that nev-er paid a shil - ling.
that nev-er paid a shil - ling.
that nev-er paid a shil - ling.
Chorus.
Lords may sip their port.
Lords may sip their port,
Lords may sip their port, Tay may do for wimmen,
Lords may sip their port, Tay may do for wimmen,
cresc.
But to fight or court, Poth-een, Poth - een's what we swim
But to fight or court, Poth-een, Poth - een's what we swim
But to fight or court, Poth-een, Poth - een's what we swim
But to fight or court, Poth-een, Poth - een's what we swim

in!   (Father O'Flynn and Nora
together near C.)

in!   (Chorus scatter themselves, lounging on the stage,
while Kitty goes round replenishing glasses;

in!   after a while Kitty wanders off R.U.E.)

in!

O'Flynn. *mp*

No - ra,   my

dim.   *p*   *pp*

Nora. *p*

O'Flynn.   What else   would they be,   and my

col - leen, your eyes __ are   dim?

boy __ a-way?

cresc.

He'll make his point, you may trust to him,   He'll be

cresc.

ad lib.

Father, oh Father,

back again ere close of day.

colla voce *trem.*

my heart ____ stands still. For the

last two nights, in the mid - night gloom, I

rall.

heard the Banshee a - keen-ing shrill, And an-

colla voce

o - - ther keen ____ is the knell of doom.

O'Flynn.

No-ra, my col-leen, your heart is sore, sure the Ban-shee wails for a hun-dred more__ Perhaps for some wand'ring stranger's sake, who's drowning now in a moun-tain lake.

Nora.

A stranger? Father, your wits have fled. Would the Banshee care if the likes were dead? Not for a stranger she'll wail and keen, but the best old stock of our E-rin green.

O'Flynn.

And you think 'tis for

Nora. *rall.*

O'Flynn.

The same as she did when his fa-ther

Shamus the Banshee cried.

Lento.

died. A grave was cold. In the churchyard mould. A

low, dark bed for the bright and bold; It op-en'd wide On the

moun - tain side The first night ev - er the Banshee cried.

No child or scion of the great O'Brien, But the

Ban - shee keens, yes, she keens when she knows him dying.

One night a sigh, and the next a cry, with the third wail

surely a man must die. The sound comes clear

to the tor - tured ear of her whom the doom'd one has loved most dear.

Twice thro' the gloom Have I heard the doom wail-ing like

women be-fore a tomb. If once more, but once

more I hear that aw--ful, aw--ful, aw-ful cry,

I'll know my Shamus is call'd to die.

O'Flynn. **Allegro moderato.**

Cheer up, cheer up,

No-ra a-roon, Shamus is safe, he'll be with you soon,

(Kitty runs on from R.)

80

Kitty.

Come, boys, come, put the glasses down!

Lynch, the pi - per, is come to town.

(♩. = ♩) (Chorus come forward. Enter the old

p

mp staccato

L.H.

piper with his pipes.)

O'Flynn. *mf*

I've

look'd up - on sor - rows of se - ver - al types, But sel - dom seen one wouldn't

yield to the pipes, When the heart is o'er-burthen'd with

5

all that it feels, Dance, Dance, Dance all the mi-se-ry

out at your heels.

Jig.
Vivace.

Repeat as often as
necessary for the dance. Last time.

Chorus.

Soprano.

Alto.

Tenor.

'Tis Sha - - mus!

Bass.

'Tis Sha - - mus!

(Shamus enters. Nora embraces him. He tears

off the old coat and hat, kisses her, and draws her forward.) **Shamus.**

The

'Tis Sha - - mus! Oh, boys, lis-ten to Sha-mus!

'Tis Sha - - mus! Oh, boys, lis-ten to Sha-mus!

'Tis Sha - - mus! Oh, boys, lis-ten to Sha-mus!

'Tis Sha - - mus! Oh, boys, lis-ten to Sha-mus!

5

Presto, ma non troppo.

sol - diers are safe for the rest of the night, with their feet in a boghole, their

head in the heather, I left them a will - o'- the wisp for a light, And

sure - ly they ought to be hap - py to - geth - er. I

took them thro' ri - vers, I took them thro' bogs with lots of great

tussocks to trip us and lame us, Ye'd laugh to have

5

seen them all pant-ing like dogs, and catch - ing a

breath to fling cur - - - ses at Sha - mus.

They're safe where they are, for I

called from the hill, "Don't stir till day - light, it's no road for a

strang - er; But if you're con - tent - ed and try to keep

still, To-mor-row will find you in no sort of dang-er."

I kissed them my hand, and I gave them a cheer, I

took the short cut by the pass of Glen-co-rah, I

wast-ed no minutes, and now I am here

For a glass of poth-een and a dance with my

Reel.

Allegro molto. (The dance is resumed. Sunset effect on the scene.)

(The piper marches off, followed by all the Chorus. Shamus draws Nora over to the bench by the 87

Chorus, (in two divisions)

Come all ye true bred I-rishmen that love a song and dance, And

house. Kitty and Father O'Flynn join them.)

give the pi-per hear-ty cheer whene'er you get the chance; Ould Ire-land, as we

know too well, has plen-ty to en-dure. But while we've poth-een, pipes and jigs, you

1ma volta
Come all ye true bred

2nda volta

cannot call us poor.   cannot call us poor

Andante tranquillo.

Nora.

I'll wake up Paudeen_ I think he's fast_

Till you give him a kiss, dear, it may be the last.

(Exit into house)

Shamus.

What ails her? The last?

O'Flynn.

Sure the girl's in a fright, The

Banshee was crying ere yes-ter-day night.

Shamus: (spoken) The Banshee!

(Enter Nora, with Paudeen in her arms)

Più lento.

Nora.

Kiss him, Sha-mus, kiss our dar-ling!

Nora.
Shamus.
'Twill be com-fort to ye, may be.
Aye, with all my heart.
Aye, if we must
part.
So you heard? Speak, asthore!
Sure I told you_
Agitato e poco accelerando.
It was the Banshee, I heard the keen Ere
Just once more!
Agitato e poco accelerando.
yesterday, last night a - gain.
rall.
But on - ly

Tempo I.

Shamus.

twice; Sure ma-ny hearsthat and ne-ver a soul goes short of breath.

Nora

But she'll keen a - gain; If the third voice

wails, 'tis de - sti-ny's call! **Lento.**

Shamus

And it means my

Lento.

Banshee (behind the scenes)

senza tempo

Ul - la, ul -la-lone, ul -la-lone_ och_ one, och- one

death.

colla voce

più f (la seconda colta ancora più f)

Ul - la, ul-la-lone, ul-la-lone och - onoohone

pp

Banshee.

pp

Ul - - la -

Nora.

pp molto espress.

Oh, my dar-lint, my

O'Flynn.

Hark, hark, 'tis the Ban - shee's cry!

pp

pp

Banshee.

3

lone, ul - la - lone ochone!

Kitty.

p

Nora.

Oh, Fa -

pride, my je - well

Shamus.

Young and strong, I have got____ to die!

92

Kitty.

- ther, oh Fa - ther, but Fate____ is cru-el!

Tempo di Marcia.

Nora.

oh Fa - ther, but Fate____ is cru-el!

Shamus.

oh Fa - ther, but Fate____ is cru-el!

O'Flynn.

oh Fa - ther, but Fate____ is cru-el!

Tempo di Marcia.

(Kitty sees the gleam of a bayonet, and lays her hand on

pp

pp

Shamus' arm, pointing up the road.)   (Shamus runs up the street and is met by a row of bayonets.)

cresc.

(The peasants pour on R. and come almost into collision with the troops, but give back before the bayonets.)

f

f

8

93

its ful-fill-ing, you'll soon be free, and I am willing, Jack for

Capt.

That's the

Jill, an' Pat for Bid-dy, I'll not lave ye long a wid-dy.

re-bel yon - - der! seize___ him!

p trem. *p cresc.*

Shamus. (surrendering)

Come, boys, a-nything to please him!

mf *cresc.*

Kitty. *sf* *sf*

Shame on ye, shame on ye, Look what you'-re doin',

mf *p staccato*

sf *sf*

Tak-ing the man with the child in his arms.
O'Flynn.
Shame on ye, bring-ing a
household to ru-in,
Tak-ing the head from the best of our farms!
p
Kitty.
Shame on ye, shame on ye!
Shame on ye, shame on ye!
Nora.
Shame on ye, shame on ye!
Shame on ye, shame on ye!
Capt.
Will you be si-lent?
O'Flynn.
Shame on ye, shame on ye!
Shame on ye, shame on ye!
Soprano.
Alto.
Shame on ye, shame on ye!
Chorus.
Tenor.
Bass.
sf
p

Capt.
Will you be si-lent? This is my du-ty, and it must be
done.
deciso
If you would on-ly keep peace in your is-land, You'd
Soprano.
Alto.
Chorus.
Shame on ye!
Tenor.
Bass
ne-ver see ei-ther bayonet or gun.
Nora.
Oh, spare his life to me! Grant me his
wife to be, Let me not live as his

Kitty.

mf

Mu-sha, it's fen - si-ble,

Nora.

wi - dow for - lorn. Oh, spare his

Sure he'll be peace-a-ble, harm - less,

life to me! Oh, spare his life to me!

harm - less as Pau - deen a - fore he was

Let me not live as his wi - dow for -

born.

lorn. Shamus.

Girls, do not cringe to him,

p

mf

5

Yield____ not an inch to him, Sure you heard death in the

Ban-shee's shrill keen. On - - ly rear

Pad - dy here Up____ like his dad - dy here, To

poco rall.

wor - - ship his coun - - try and die for____ the

Mike. *mf*

Don't be cast down then, my colleen as - tho - ra, I'll____ be your

Green.

Kitty.

(Nora raises her head, as if to reply to Mike, but falls

Mike.

Spit on him, spurn at him, tramp on him,

friend when your Sha - mus is gone!

Kitty.

fainting, into Father O'Flynn's arms.)

No - ra!

Capt.

Si - lence, you blackguard, your por - tion is done.

Shamus.

rall.

Dar -

Poco più lento.

molto espress.

- ling, a - dieu to you! Sure my heart flew to you

E - ven when tak - ing the sword in my hand.

Kit-ty, be good to her! Fa-ther, you've stood to her.

Stand to her still when I'm out of the land.

O'Flynn.

Cheer up, for

Capt.

Take off the pri-so-ner!

Shamus.

Good-bye, my gos-

life is in her!

soon grow up like a man!

Molto più lento.
Kitty.
molto espress.
Don't fret a - bout her, dear! Don't
fret with - out her, dear!
fp
f
Col Ped.
Tempo di marcia.
I'll bring you news of her just as I can!
f
(Soldiers commence to hurry Shamus off. The villagers rush forward and throw themselves on the
ff
Troops. A brief struggle. Sergeant is compelled to let Shamus go. He flings himself between the opposing ranks.)
Stand back!

ad lib.
a tempo animato
Home, boys! Save your-selves, and save your hearths!
Sop.
Alto.
Ten.
Bass.
Chorus.
You've got one
colla voce
pri-son-er, hold him fast for he's the last you'll get, But,
ff
by the rock of Cashel! you haven't hung him

(Shamus is dragged off by Soldiers. Kitty bending over Nora, who is fainting in Father O'Flynn's arms. The Peasantry following the Soldiers to entrance with uplifted sticks, and Mike Murphy cow-

yet!

yet!

yet!

yet!

ering close beside the Captain)

End of Act I.

Nº 9. Entracte.

Andante.

5

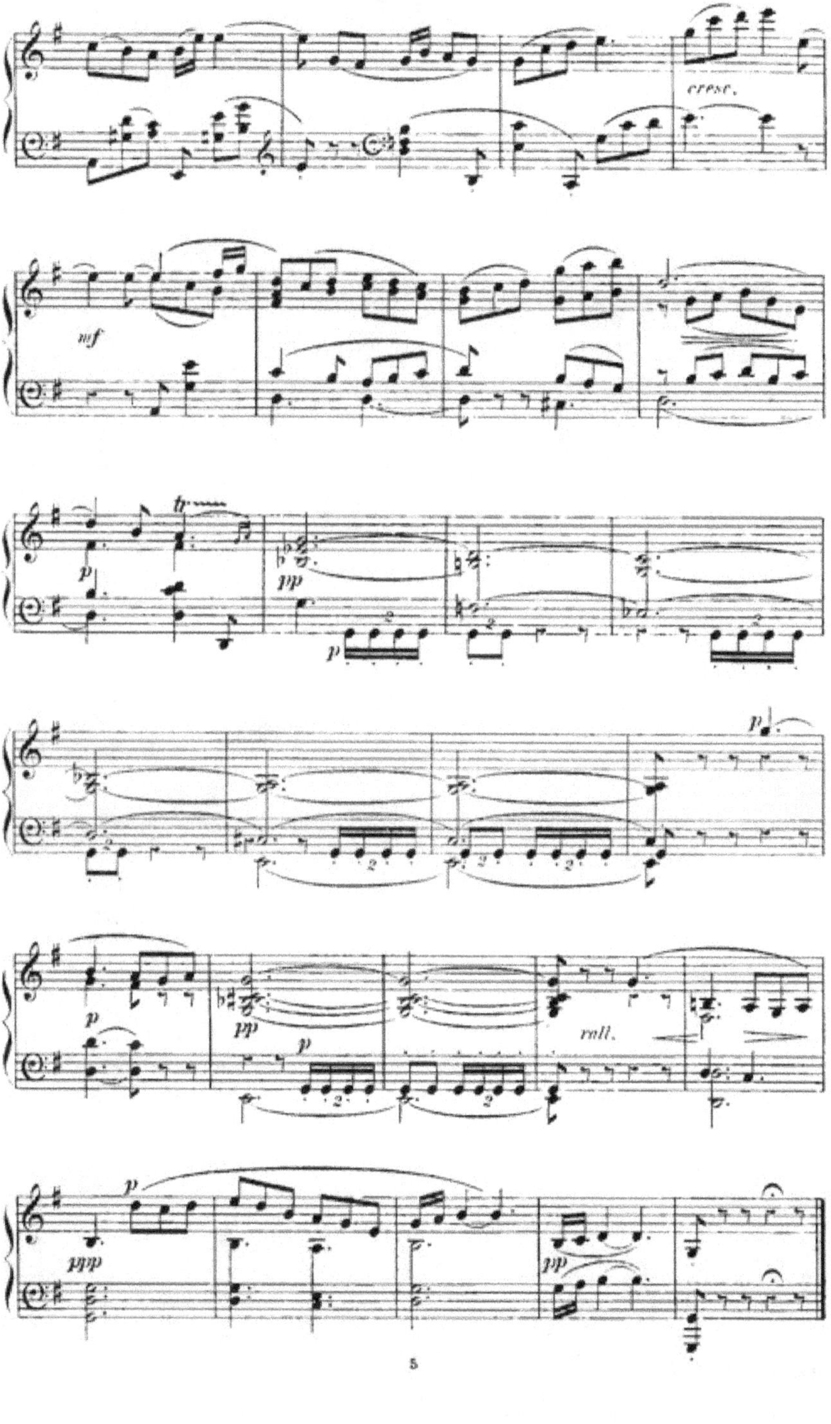
cresc.
mf
tr
p
pp
p
p
p
pp
p
rall.
p
ppp
pp

Act II.

Scene I. — The Barrack Square. Practicable door in porch R., leading to the military lock-up. Entrances R.U.E. and L.U.E. Main entrance L. 2 and 3 E. A broad entrance, this all set obliquely so as to show a part of the road beyond, leading to main gate. A sentry box at either side of this entrance. The relief round, led by Sergeant Cox, enters R.U.E. and marches to each entrance with military music, changing the guard. They are about to march off when Captain Trevor enters L.U.E., sentry saluting.

Nº 10. Introduction.

Alla marcia.

N.B. The rising of the Curtain must be timed so as to finish the change of guard, and begin the dialogue at the point indicated. This must vary according to the size of the stage.

5

mf
cresc.
f
dim.
(Captain Trevor enters)
p
Captain "I want to speak to you, Sergeant & c"
Serg: ...
Serg. "Right face, Quick march!"
right, sir.
pp morendo
ppp
R.H.

Nọ 11 Solo. Captain.
Andante moderato.

But demmit
. . . . rebel.

It's deuced hard lines!

I can't let him go __ I can't give her up __ What the de - vil can I

do? My heart is thrall to Kitty's beauty, And honour

rall.

points the path of du - ty, A - las! a - las! they can't a-

gree. If Shamus dies, she can but hate me; If he survives,what tri - als wait me! A - las, a - las, and woe is

me! woe is me! The re-bel must not be for-given, the

fair, bright maid, with eyes like heaven, must weep and suf-fer

all thro' me. Oh, for the power to solve these puzzles, to snatch

him from the levelled muzzles, and set him free, and set him

free! Oh, were I not a British
sol-dier, I'd give up all, so I might hold your soft hand in mine,
all fan - cy free! But ere you will con-sent to marry, I must dis-
grace the sword I car-ry. It cannot be, it cannot be! it can - not
be! No! A - dieu, a - dieu, my mountain
p
fp
pp
mp
f
molto espr.
dim.
Ped.

fai - ry. Your heart is soft. but will not va - ry its stern de-

cree. its stern de - cree. I turn my back on love and

beau - ty. This thorn - y path the path of du -

Più lento.

ty Leads far from thee, far far from thee!

(cue) Sergeant It will soon be sunrise.

Nᵒ 12. Duet. Captain and Mike.

Moderato con moto.

(Mike follows the Captain, trying to pluck his sleeve)

What the devil are you do-ing?

If your no-ble ho-nour pla-zes, 'Tis a-bout that small re-wardment.

You and it may go to bla-zes! Have I got it in my pocket? Sure, I thought it's

Well, the Government pro-claimed it, And they're apt you might.

5

sure to make it right! So dont get so flurried! The Crown won't be
But I am so flur-ried!

hur-ried To please an im - pa-tient, bog-trot-ting spal-peen,
The Crown wont be hur - ried To please an im - pa-tient spal-

You'll get all your money. Then wont it be fun-ny, to say___ you've had debts___
peen. If they'll pay me the money. Then wont it be funny to say I've had

___ from the King and the Queen?___
debts from the King and the Queen?___ Oh___ yer

Allegretto.

Mike.

honour, dont be hard, But a - bout that same re-ward, I can't do with-out it at

all, __ at all. And Go-vern-ment, I'm told, Is __ loth to part with gold, And I

Capt

And I think you're not to blame I'm

dare - nt stay lon-ger near Glen - gall, Glen-gall.

glad you've so much shame. For they'll skin you if they catch you in Glen-

No. 1

5

gall. Glen - gall.

da-rent stay lon-ger near Glen-gall. Glen-gall. Just —

dim *p*

think of all I've done. And all the risks I've run, And en - tire-ly Cap-tain, for your

p

Più lento.

a tempo

sake, your sake, His rev-er-ence looks black, And my col-leen turns her back, And the

colla voce *mf* *p* *p a tempo*

Capt.

mf

And I

neigh-bours re-gard me as a snake. a snake. ___

pp

5

think they're nearly right. Though your skin's not over bright. In calling you a serpent, no mis-

Yes, the

take, mis - take!

neighbours re-gard me as a snake, a snake. ____ So you

see I've lost my girl, Set the village in a whirl, And, may-be, done damage to my

rall. Più lento.

soul, my soul. I took ye from the bog. I've hun-ted like a dog, Don't

Tempo I.
f più
Faith. I
accel.
lave me un-re-war-ded at the goal. the goal.
accel.
animato
take but lit-tle pride in standing at your side. If you call yourself a win-ner on the
Don't
p
whole. the whole!
If you call yourself a
lave me un-re-war-ded at the goal. the goal.
Don't
cresc.
mp
f
f
Più mosso.
win - ner on the whole.
lave me unrewarded at the goal.
f
8

Nº 13 Solo Mike.

Andante.

Mike.

mf

Och - one, when I used to be

rall.   *a tempo*   *f*

young, och - one when I used to be young! Them was the days I was

colla parte

free and hear-ty, The life and soul of a dan - cing par-ty, the first boy

poco rall.

axed when a song was sung! Och - one, when I used to be

colla parte

a tempo

young! Then I could court as sweet as honey; Di-vil a hair I thought of money, och sure I was brave— and young.

Och - one, when I used to be young!—

p poco rall.

calla parte

f

Più mosso.

Now look at me, poor and bat-ter'd, Can - een patch'd and coat all tat-ter'd,

Look at the work of a wo - - man's tongue! Born from the kings that

ruled the pa-rish, Sure a-ny Girl should be proud of marriage wid the

5

Tempo I.

oul-dest stock she lived a - mong. Och - one! Och - one, when I used to be

young, used to be young! The fai - ries danced at my

mo - ther's marryin', The Ban - shee keen'd

— at my fa - ther's berry-in, The

wild - - est keen that e - ver she sung!

5

Sure all the world has turn'd a-gin me, Since No-ra scorn'd the love with

in me wid a could sharp 'No' from her cru-el tongue.

Più lento.

Ochone! Ochone! Ochone!

Ochone!— Och — - one when I used to be young! Ochone! Och-one! when I

used to be young! Ochone!

Nº 14. Ensemble. Kitty. Chorus of Peasants and Soldiers.

Andante con moto.

(off the stage)

Soprani. *mf*

Walk. _____ girls.

Alti. *mf*

Walk. _____ girls.

Andante con moto.

Sergeant "Hark!

walk. _____ here's the man _____ we all are proud of. Sure, a

walk. _____ here's the man _____ we all are proud of. Sure, a

What's that?"

word or two of talk is the most _____ we'll be al-lowed of. _____

word or two of talk is the most _____ we'll be al-lowed of. _____

Sing. _____ girls. sing. _____ Sure per-

Sing. _____ girls. sing. _____ Sure per-

5

haps he'll hear __ us __ singing; Och, 'twould be an-oth-er thing. if

haps he'll hear __ us __ singing; Och, 'twould be an-oth-er thing. if

Kitty. (Kitty and a band of Peasant Girls appear at entrance L. the Sentries bar the way.)

Och. you're a soldier. handsome and

com - fort we were bringing! __

com - fort we were bringing! __

great; Sure __ ye won't keep us here at the gate. __ Time's

short I'm say-in' it, Now you're de-lay-in' it; Put up that bayonet Don't make us

wait. 'Tis yer-
Chorus. With yer beau-ti-ful scar-let coats And yer swords an' muskets bright. 'Tis yer-
(petting the Soldiers.)
With yer beau-ti-ful scar-let coats And yer swords an' muskets bright. 'Tis yer-
selves are feelin' yer oats This il-li-gant Fri-day night.
selves are feel - in' yer oats This il-li-gant Fri-day night.
selves are feel - in' yer oats This il-li-gant Fri-day night. Acush-la ma-
A-cushla ma-chree! Sure ye wouldn't touch me. And as quick as a
chree! I'm as smart as a flea, and as quick as a

sprite!

sprite!

(The Girls dart past the Sentries, who vainly endeavour to stop them)

Kitty (sings, going up to Sergeant C.)

Ar-rah, Sergeant asthore. Sure you will not be cross! Think

poco rall **Poco più lento.**

all we have bore. And remember our loss. For it's not in yer beau-ti-ful eye. An' it's

not in yer smil-ing face. To put us asthray, or to turn us a-way. When we've

ven-tured here to your place. You won't mis-name us. You

could - n't blame us, We must see Sha - mus,

And face ____ to face. ____

The red coat, the red coat, the pret-ti-est coat that

The red coat, the red coat, the pret-ti-est coat that

ev - er was seen; But a dread coat, a dread coat, 'Tis my-self would like for to

ev - er was seen; But a dread coat, a dread coat, 'Tis my-self would like for to

paint it green. Sure a - ny dress, as long as it co-vers a

paint it green. But a - ny dress, as long as it co-vers a

p cresc. f
man - ly heart. Can do no less, can feel no less than shame at
man - ly heart. Can do no less, can feel no less than shame at
cresc.
Soprani.
keep-ing true friends a - part.
Alti.
keep-ing true friends a - part.
Tenori.
Well, my girls, we
Bassi.
Well, my girls, we
f
won't be cru - el. So you are not cru - el las - ses. You shall see your
won't be cru - el. So you are not cru - el las - ses. You shall see your
p
f
vil-lage je - wel. See him thro' our can - teen glas - ses.
vil-lage je - wel. See him thro' our can - teen glas - ses.

Tho' you mayn't think with us. Still, you can drink with us. This poor old

Tho' you mayn't think with us, Still, you can drink with us. This poor old

barrack has got its can-teen. Good British ale an' beer. Noth - ing is

barrack has got its can-teen. Good British ale an' beer. Noth - ing is

fai-lin here, Not e'en a drop of your na - tive po - theen.

fai-lin here, Not e'en a drop of your na - tive po - theen.

Più lento.

A friendly hand in for - eign land. What e - ver tint your coat is painted.

Chorus. A friendly hand in for - eign land. What e - ver tint your coat is painted.

A friendly hand in for - eign land. What e - ver tint your coat is painted,

A friendly hand in for - eign land. What e - ver tint your coat is painted,

Più lento.

5

Tempo I.

Will bring good cheer, will bring good cheer,

Will bring good cheer will bring good cheer,

Will bring good cheer will bring good cheer, for a glass of

Will bring good cheer will bring good cheer, for a glass of

Tempo I.

mf

And a glass of whis-ky are well ac-quaint - ed.

And a glass of whis-ky are well ac-quaint - ed.

beer are well ac-quaint - ed.

beer are well ac-quaint - ed.

cresc.

ff

dim. (Exeunt Soldiers and Girls R.U.E.) *dim.*

p

p   *pp*   *pp dim.*   *morendo*   (Enter Captain.)

130

(Cue) Kitty: "mind kissing you,—if—

Nº 15. Duet. Kitty and Captain.

Molto moderato.

Captain. "it what?" Kitty. "Oh, its a very cautious 'if' entirely."

Kitty.

So it's kis-ses you're craving, You big soldier man!

But first quit your mis-be-hav-ing, and I know you can.

Not that I'm afeared of kissin'. I'm not prim nor stiff,

But be-fore I yield or listen, There's a cau-tious "if";

Copyright 1896 by Boosey & Cº

3

Kitty.
Captain.
Poco più mosso.
There's a cau-tious "if." It's a mighty lit-tle
It's a
Poco più mosso.
word, but I've of-ten read and heard it makes us all the
mighty lit-tle word but I've of-ten read and heard it
trouble, all the trouble that it can. I've a right to ask at
makes us all the trouble that it can. You've a right to ask at
feast, if you've spread the wedding feast, if you've called up-on the
feast, if I've spread the wedding feast if I've called up-on the

priest. My big soldier man, my big soldier man.

priest, Like a sol - dier man, like a sol - dier man.

Kitty.

I can kiss by easy sta-ges as the love birds do;

But you'll tell me where the cage is, Ere I hop to you. You must

cresc.

tell me if you can, sir, how you mean to live For be -

fore you get my answer, There's a cau-tious "if." There's a

cau - tious "if!" I'm as proud as a - ny

You're as proud as a - ny Duchess, and be -

Duchess and be - fore your lip as much as ei - ther cheek or fore-head

fore my lip as much as ei - ther cheek or fore - head

tou - ches in a kiss from you, your pro -

tou - ches in a kiss for you, my pro -

po - sal you must write it, and I'll have my friends in - vi - ted, and I'll

po - sal I must write it, and you'll have your friends in - vi - ted, and you'll

5

see the chapel lighted, and the ring in view, and the

see the chapel lighted, and the ring in view, and the

mf *p*

ring in view.

ring in view. You're as charming as an English spring, you're as

pp *mp*

(imitating him.)

You're stray - ing from th'im-por-tant thing,

dain - ty as a milk white pearl!

p

leggiero

Don't try blarney with an I-rish girl! *mf espress.*

It's ve-ry hard, my darl - ing

pp

Kit - ty, To be de - barred from lips so pretty. The tide now
flows,_____ But per - chance the ebb'll Fling my heart close at your
feet, close at your feet, fair rebel, fair rebel!

pp
pp

Kitty.

Capt. So we'll wait a lit - tle longer, Say a

So we'll wait a lit - tle longer, Say a week or two,_____ and if

week or two, and if love keeps growing stronger, Why, I'll hop to you _____

and if love keeps growing stronger. Why, I'll

And we'll

hop to you And we'll ba-nish all suggestion of a

banish all suggestion of a tiff, a tiff. a tiff. Till we've

tiff, a tiff, a tiff. Till we've

rall.

solved the mighty question of this cau-tious "if."

solved the mighty question of this cau-tious "if,"

of this cau - tious "if."

of this cau - tious "if."

Nº 16. Duet. Nora, Shamus.

Tempo di Marcia.

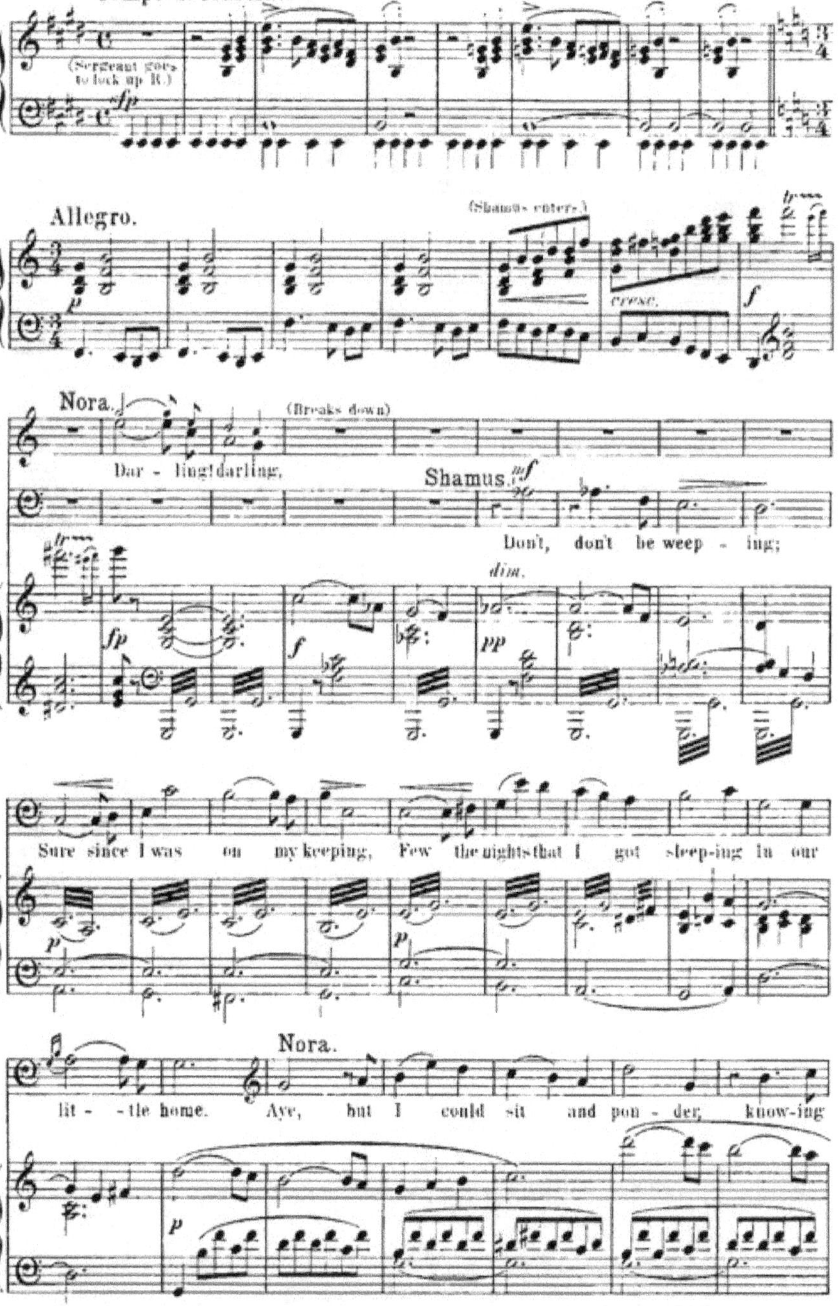

far — as you — night wan - der, you were some - where

Nora.

ov - er you - - der. and you'd sure - ly come,

Shamus.

Dar - - ling,

Dar - ling, Nev - - er-

Nev - - er-

more! ____ when ev' - ning falls, will I rise when

more! ____ when ev' - ning falls, will she rise when

pp
Sha - mus calls, nev - er - more!
pp
Sha - mus calls, nev - er - more!
più f
nev - er - more within those walls
più f
nev - er - more within those walls
shall I hear your tread.
shall you hear my tread.
mf
f
Oh, that cru - el
f
Oh, that cru - el

Ban - shee's wail nev - - er told a tru - - er

Ban - shee's wail nev - - er told a tru - - er

tale; Will she nev - er, nev - er fail? Will she

tale; Will she

mf *p* *mf* *p*

nev - er, nev - er fail? Must she

nev - er, nev - er fail? Must she

p *p*

pp *p* *colla voce*

have her dead?

have her dead?

pp

Animato. ♪. più mosso che ♩)

Shamus.

Come, girl, now my on - ly, on - ly me - rit is to

show that I in - he - rit some - thing of my fa - ther's spi - - -

Nora. *f*

Love, _____ it is your life.

rit!

Dar - - - ling, how my head is swimming, Dar - - ling,

see, my eyes are dim - ming;

142

Shamus.

Show ___ your - self ___ the pearl ___ of wo - men

Prove ___ your self my wife. ___

Allegro.

Nora.

Let   us   face   the   foe - men   bold - ly,   Let us

Shamus.

Let   us   face   the   foe - men   bold - ly,   Let us

Allegro.

meet   them   stern - - ly,   cold - - - - ly,   One   soft

meet   them   stern - - ly,   cold - - - ly,   One   soft

glance and whis-per on - - - ly shared by you and

glance and whis-per on - - ly shared by you and

me. Life's a bat - - tle; We have

me. Life's a bat - - tle; We have

lost it, Re - ckon not how much it cost - -

lost it, Re - ckon not how much it cost - -

- - ed! Death's a riv - er,

- - ed! Death's a riv - er,

5

144

When we've crost it, You shall wait for me, Dar-ling! You shall wait for me Dar-ling! Dar-ling! I shall wait for thee!

When we've crost it,

I shall wait for thee, dar-ling!

I shall wait for thee! Dar-ling!

Dar-ling! I shall wait for thee!

trem.
fpp
(Captain appears at L. U. E. Kitty and Father following)
(Capt Guards, remove &c.)
pp
(Shamus embraces Nora and is led off by the Sergeant Nora sinks on the stage, covering her face.)
Più lento.
O'Flynn. p
Tranquillo
pp
R. H.
Leave her lone-ly with her sor-row; There are times when friend-ly words Hurt us ev-en more than bit-ter; She is fee-ling how it hurts.
L. H.
R. H.
pp

(Cor. Mike."Close to the gallows this time.")

N.º 17. Ensemble and Melodrama.

(Bugle Call for Officers)

(The Captain and officers enter. A line of Soldiers is drawn up behind. The Peasants girls enter, also Father O'Flynn and Kitty, who draw Nora to them, leaving Mike alone. The

Tempo di Marcia.

officers take their places behind the drums.)

(The Captain fixes

Captain "The court
is open - - - - -
- - - - little room
for doubt in this case"

5

Allegro.
(Captain consults officers in dumb show)
(all indicate assent)
Captain "Shamus. . . . . . . tried."
Shamus "That word . . . . . lied."
Captain "The sentence . . . is"
Nora. agitato
Have mer - cy, your ho-nour, oh, don't say the word, don't say the word!
He's all that I have, and so young, kind gen-tle-men, try to for-get what you've heard, sure he al-ways was rash with his

tongue, spare him, your ho-nour. spare him, spare! That is a
Sopr.
Chorus.
Spare him!
Alt.
dim.
grief I could not bear.
Spare him, the re-bel-lious
All the re-bels fly to cov-er. Hearths are
ov-er

cold and hearts are bro - - - ken, Leave the words of death un-

spo - ken! By the po - wer that he braved_ Save _____ him, as you would be

Nora. *rall.*
Save him, as you would be saved!

Capt. *mf*
I grieve to say_

Shamus. *f*
Oh, wait a bit!

saved! (They kneel.)

Shamus.
Don't kneel down to a thing like it! I'm grieved, heart-sore, to leave my
wife, but I wouldn't take a gift of life!
O'Flynn.
Sha - mus, my
son.
Moderato.
Capt.
Have done, have done, 'tis a pain - ful du - ty I must ful -
fil.
Silence in
Sopran.
Chorus.
But-cher! But-cher! of course you will! But-cher! But-cher!
Alt.
cresc.

court! Ser - geant, sup - port your of - fi - cers! Cut this ri - o - ting

(The soldiers push back the peasants.)

short!

Shamus.

Oh! let the

gen - tle - man have his say! I can't be wait - ing on him all

day!

Lento.

O'Flynn

God rest his spir - it!

Lento.

Capt. "The court's decision ... hanged as a rebel"

(The Officers rise and leave the stage)

5

Sopran.
mf cresc.
Peasants.
No, no, no, we can nev - er part you so.
Alt.
mf cresc.
No, no, no, no, no, no! we can nev - er part you so. You're a
Tenor.
mf
Soldiers.
Ho! ho! ho! He's the
Bass.
mf
Ho! ho! ho! ho! ho! ho! He's the chap, the
p
You're a gift we can - - - not give, There'll be
gift you're a gift we can - - - not give, There'll be
chap that fooled us so, through low bog and moun - tain high.
chap that fooled us so, through low bog and moun - tain high.
res - cue for your wife's sake, there'll be res - cue for your life's sake, you shall
res - cue for your wife's sake, there'll be res - cue for your life's sake, you shall
When the morn - ing bells are clang - ing, we shall have a pret - ty
When the morn - ing bells are clang - ing, we shall have a pret - ty
cresc.

End of Act II Scene I.

Scene II.   A country road winding across stage. Behind road a hill, studded with trees. L. a mossy bank.

Nº 18. Chorus and Ensemble. Nora. Kitty. Father O'Flynn.

Allegro.

(A number of peasants run down road from L to R. Then Chorus of Peasants Enter from L.)

They're tak - ing him from the jail, bound —

They're tak - ing him from the jail, bound —

They're tak - ing him from the jail, bound —

They're tak - ing him from the jail, bound —

— and without re - sis - tance. Sha - mus, we will not fail, we're

— and without re - sis - tance. Sha - mus, we will not fail, we're

— and without re - sis - tance. Sha - mus, we will not fail, we're

— and without re - sis - tance. Sha - mus, we will not fail, we're

5

com-ing to your as - sis - - - tance.
com-ing to your as - sis - - tance.
com-ing to your as - - sis - - - tance.
com-ing to your as - sis - - - tance. We'll show them which is which, we'll
cresc.
we'll show them which is which, we'll leave them in the
we'll show them which is which, we'll leave them in the ditch in the
we'll show them which is which, we'll leave them in the
leave them in the ditch, we'll show them which is which, we'll leave them in the ditch, in the
ditch, we'll bring back Sha-mus to Bal-ly-ha-mis! and
ditch, we'll bring back Sha-mus to Bal-ly-ha-mis! and
ditch, we'll bring back Sha-mus to Bal-ly-ha-mis! and
ditch, we'll bring back Sha-mus to Bal-ly-ha-mis! and

(They run off)

learn them which is which. Sha - - mus we will not fail!

learn them which is which. Sha - - mus we will not fail!

(The men wave their

learn them which is which. Sha - -

learn them which is which. Sha - -

dim.

blackthorns as they go.)

- - mus we will not fail!

- - mus we will not fail!

p

Father O'Flynn and Kitty enter from L. supporting Nora between them.
She carries Paudeen in her arms.)

Lento.

pp

p express.

5

Nora.
This is the place, fa-ther.
O'Flynn.
Here he must pass.
Wait here, poor stricken souls, rest on the grass.
Kitty.
To take our last look of poor Shamus.
Nora.
A-las! Oh! a-
Andante.
Kitty.
'Twas only a week a-go this beautiful sum- - mer
Nora.
las!
'Twas only a week a-go this beautiful sum- - mer
O'Flynn.
'Twas only a week a-go this beautiful sum- - mer
Andante.

wea - ther, we walked the fields we used to sow, when we all were happy to-
wea - ther, we walked the fields we used to sow, when we all were happy to-
wea - ther, we walked the fields we used to sow, when we all were happy to-
ge - ther. And now we wait the stroke of fate from
ge - ther. And now we wait the stroke of fate from
ge - ther. And now we wait the stroke of fate from
men we hate; To whom life is a cheap as a feather.
men we hate; To whom life is a cheap as a feather.
men we hate; To whom life is a cheap as a feather.

Nora. Sha - mus, my life, Sha-mus, my life in a-no-ther hour he'll be lost to his wife; He'll be past the power of love to wake him.

O'Flynn. My child, take heed! your tears will shake him, your sobs will break him, and he has need of cou-rage and

Kitty. Oh! he will not swerve, he will not swerve from the path he's nerve.

5

Kitty
cho - sen without re - serve! A woman's
Nora.
A woman's
O'Flynn.
A woman's
cresc.
tear, a wo-mans tear, it is our on - ly off' - - ring
tear, a wo-mans tear, it is my on - ly off' - - ring
tear, a wo-mans tear, it is her on - ly off' - - ring
here; 'Twill fall un - heed - ed on the bier of all she has to love and
here; 'Twill fall un - heed - ed on the bier of all I have to love and
here; 'Twill fall un - heed - ed on the bier of all she has to love and

trust! A fare - well sobbed, a last em - brace, A

cling - ing kiss up - on his face, _____ Then turn we

to the bu - rial place, to learn our les - son,

Lento.

"Dust to dust!"

"Dust to dust!"

"Dust to dust!"

Lento.

p espress.

pp

Father.

The time draws closer, Kit-ty, guard her well, for this one hour 'tis Shamus needs me

pp

pp

(Exit R.)

most.

pp

Più mosso. *mf* **Nora.**

Smile, boy, smile, we have had e-nough of woe, Father's

p

coming, Father's coming by - and-bye, you shall see him go.

p

Più lento.

Kitty.

Nora.

No-ra, you frighten the

Go, go, go to his aw-ful doom!

child, Nora, your looks are wild!

Think of the empty room,

Think of the de-solate hearth; Think of the or-phan

boy, Think of the smiles and joy that centred around his

Kitty.

No-ra, he'll live to for-get, Nora, he's on-ly a ba-by yet.

birth.

Lento moderato.
(Nora kisses the child wildly and then looks dazed)
Nora. p
And we are a-
lone on earth.
f
pp
p espress.
Enter Mike. M. "Well, girls, . . .
Kitty. . . Take heart and be brave darling"
Nº 19. Finale.
Tempo di Marcia.
Sopr.
Alto. Chorus. (behind the scenes.)
Tempo di Marcia.
(very distant)
mf
Side Drum.
very distant at first.
continued until the asterisk on P. 169
Kitty. "I can hear them coming now"
(distant)
Ulla-
p

Nora.
p
Hark! hark! 'tis the Banshee a - gain!
lone! ullalone! och - one and ochone! The beau - tiful face and the
och - one and ochone! The beau - tiful face and the
p
I hear her screeching, grasping reaching for the lives
fear - less eye! Och-one al-la-la, my
fear - less eye! my
Kitty.
Si - ster, no, the Banshee wailed
the lives of men!
own. my own! oh, why must you die, oh, why must you die?
own. my own! oh, why must you die, oh why must you die?

thrice before this fa - tal hour.
Ne - ver has her warning
failed; Heav'n protect us from her power! This la -
ment upris - ing, dying. Thro' the val - leys in - ter -
ven - ing, 'tis our strick - en neigh-bours cry - ing, 'tis the
voice of friends a - keen - - - ing.
Sopr.
(nearer)
Ulla -
Alt.

Nora.

Sister dar - ling.

lone _____ ullalone och - one _____ and ochone. och - one _____ och -

och - one _____ and ochone. och - one _____ och -

pp

stand apart! Oh, that mourn - ful dead - ly

one.

one.

drum - ming! Every foot - fall wounds my heart, for my

boy is com - - ing, com - - ing.

I lit-tle thought ev-er a day should rise when the

step of my Sha - mus, drawing nigher, should freeze up my life-blood and

cresc.

cresc. poco a poco

scorch my eyes, like a bolt of ice and a flame of

(Enter from R. a file of soldiers, surrounded by villagers. Then an Officer, then the cart with Shamus bound on it. Father O'Flynn, walking at his side. Then Captain Trevor, followed by another detachment of military.)

fire.

Ulla - lone! ullalone! Och-

Chorus.

Ulla - lone! Och-

Ulla - lone! Och-

Ulla - lone! Ochone___ and ochone the beau - tiful face___ and the fear - - less eye, Och-

one___ and ochone the beau - tiful face___ and the fear - - less eye, Och-

one! the beau - tiful face___ and the fear - - less eye, Och-

one! the beau - tiful face___ and the fear - - less eye, Och-

one___ ul-la-la! my own, my own, oh, why ___must you die, oh,

one my own, my own, oh, why ___must you die, oh,

one my own, my own, oh, why ___must you die, oh,

one my own, my own, oh, why ___must you die, oh,

why must you die? Och-one!

why must you die? Och-one!

why must you die? Och-one!

why must you die? Och-one!

(Father O'Flynn raising his hand, and checking the man leading the cart.)

5

side Drum ceases here +)

Captain.
Wherefore?
Father O'Flynn.
I beg the favour of a moments halt. To pray and soothe this parting
sf colla voce
p
Captain.
f
I'll grant you time for prayers upon the gallows.
Shamus.
A use-less favour!
soul.
Not there?
He will not be there. Not there. Good friend and holy priest, you'll grant my
p
p
prayer. You'll be at No-ra's side?
Sopr.
Alto.
Chorus.
f
Ulla-lone! ullalone! och-one and ochone! och-
Och-one and ochone! och-
p
f
dim.

Father.

Captain, you won't refuse! Consider, please!

one och - one.

one och - one.

(Captain hesitates, Kitty comes forward swiftly and lays her hand on his arm looking in his face.)

Captain. *f*   **Più lento.**

I hardly know. Ground muskets! Stand at ease.

Shamus.

Listen to

me, men; I'll be short-ly go-ing where I'll know more than all the world is

knowing; But before entering that dark domin - ion perhaps you'd like to hear my last o -

5

Allegro molto e con brio.
pinion. I love my ould Ireland, and sure ye can't
blame me, I've fed on her legends, I've chant-ed her songs; The name that I
bear, if I failed her, would shame me, I weep o'er her woes, and I burn at her wrongs.
I've fought and I've fallen; I've heard the dread warning That told me my life must be yielded ere
night; Yet though you must kill me this beautiful morning, There's stuff in your hearts that will
mf
cresc.
f
mp
p

own I am right____ With my pike in my hand and my foot on the heather, I'd fight you a-gain as I fought you be-fore; But now I'll for-give ye the whole lot to-gether, And own that my fate is the fortune of war.____ I'm tell-ing you this____ on the road to the gallows, Not a shake in my voice, not a tear in my eye,

Nora. Allegro agitato.

Here, Shamus, here! I'm coming to you, dear, I

I'm not conquer'd yet — (He suddenly sees Nora who has risen to her feet and comes forward with Paudeen. Shamus breaks down and leans against the side of

want your last sigh, the last look of your eye, and the boy God bless him! I'll

the cart.)

nev - - er un - dress him and see him kneel to his

prayers, But his fa - . . - ther's name shall be

in the same and a curse _____ up-on his

slayers!
O'Flynn.
Hush, No-ra, hush! Ven-geance is sharp and swift; but a wrapon too
p
keen for wo - men or men, 'Tis on - ly for God to
p
lift.
Ul-la-la!
Chorus.
Och-one my own, my own, oh, why must you die, oh,
f
dim.
ff
why must you die? why must you die?
pp
dim.

Andante espressivo.

Shamus.

Raise him, No - ra, till I kiss him,

(She raises child for him to kiss.)

See how I am tied! *molto espress.*

Bloo-dy war and dead-ly schism force___ me from your

side. Once more and once more,

rall.

and a parting kiss for your-self, As-thore!

colla voce

5

Allegro molto.

On-ly one! no! no more! O'- Bri - en must keep his

colla voce

Capt.

Come fa-ther, come fa-ther! We can't be lin - ger-ing here all

pride!

day. There's your penitent... Do your office! Say whatever you've got to say.

(Father O'Flynn climbs into cart.)

I'l-la-

Chorus.

I'l-la-

I'l-la-

I'l-la-

cresc.

cresc.

5

lone ul-la-lone och-one and och-one! the beau-ti-ful face and the
lone och-one and och-one! the beau-ti-ful face and the
8va bassa
fear-less eye, och-one ul-la-la, my own, my own, Oh,
fear-less eye, och-one my own, my own, Oh,
dim.
ff
8va bassa
why must you die? oh, why must you die?
p
dim.
ppp
8va bassa

Allegro molto.
Kitty.
(Father O'Flynn cuts the ropes which bind Shamus with one stroke of his knife.)
He's free! He's a-
O'Flynn.
(Shamus leaps from the cart, knocking down
I can't stand it! Save yourself!
two soldiers R. and L. and makes for the hill, Mike comes from behind tree and tries to stop him. The soldiers are hampered by the people
Allegro molto.
and cannot fire.)
Captain "Stop him... aim low!"
foot! Now stand to him, neigh-bours!
Shamus.
(goes)
Good-bye to you, Captain, good-bye to your men!
Volley
(Pause to be held until the volley is over.)
(The soldiers fire a volley up the hill. Mike falls and rolls down the slope, Shamus is left standing at the top.)
(Off.)
When you
Oh, boys, lis-ten to Shamus!
Oh, boys, lis-ten to Shamus!
Chorus.
Oh, boys, lis-ten to Shamus!
Oh, boys, lis-ten to Shamus!
(The soldiers scatter over the hill in pursuit.)

next want a guide you'll em - ploy me a - gain!
pp
Oh, boys, lis-ten to Sha-mus!
pp
Oh, boys, lis-ten to Sha-mus!
pp
Oh,
pp
Oh,
Kitty.
mf
I'm thinking he's vanished clean out of your ken
Nora.
mf
I'm thinking he's vanished clean out of your ken
O'Flynn.
mf
I'm thinking he's vanished clean out of your ken
mp
I'm
mp
I'm
cresc.
boys, lis-ten to Sha - mus!
mp
I'm
cresc.
boys, lis-ten to Sha - mus!
mp
I'm
p

To - night he'll be sleeping in
To - night he'll be sleeping in
To - night he'll be sleeping in
think-ing he's vani-shed clean out of your ken,
think-ing he's vani-shed clean out of your ken,
think-ing he's vani-shed clean out of your ken,
think-ing he's vani-shed clean out of your ken,
p
A - her - low glen and the devil's in the dice if you catch him a - gain!
A - her - low glen and the devil's in the dice if you catch him a - gain!
A - her - low glen and the devil's in the dice if you catch him a - gain!
sf
And the
And the
And the
And the
stacc.

Search,
Search,
Search,
de-vil's in the dice if you catch him a-gain! Search,
de-vil's in the dice it you catch him a-gain! Search,
de-vil's in the dice if you catch him a-gain! Search,
de-vil's in the dice if you catch him a-gain! Search,
cresc.
boys, search af-ter Sha-mus! Search, boys, search af-ter Sha-mus! Search!
boys, search af-ter Sha-mus! Search, boys, search af-ter Sha-mus! Search!
boys, search af-ter Sha-mus! Search, boys, search af-ter Sha-mus! Search!
boys, search af-ter Sha-mus! Search boys, search af-ter Sha-mus! Search!
boys, search af-ter Sha-mus! Search boys, search af-ter Sha-mus! Search!
boys, search af-ter Sha-mus! Search boys, search af-ter Sha-mus! Search!
boys, search af-ter Sha-mus! Search boys, search af-ter Sha-mus! Search!

Search! Search! search af - ter him well!

Search! Search! search af - ter him well!

Search! Search! search af - ter him well!

Search! Search! search af - ter him well!

Search! Search! search af - ter him well!

Search! Search! search af - ter him well!

Search! Search! search af - ter him well!

(curtain)

End of the Opera.
January, 1895.

5

www.ingramcontent.com/pod-product-compliance
Lightning Source LLC
Chambersburg PA
CBHW020535270326
41927CB00006B/586